PASSION'S PROGRESS

The **C. S. Lewis Centre** is an international network of Christians from many different churches and traditions. Despite their differences, they are united by their commitment to historic Christianity.

There are a number of ways in which we work to achieve our aims. These include:

Dialogue The Centre is a meeting point for Christians who would never normally talk to each other. We make it possible for people from a rich diversity of Christian traditions to engage in open, frank debate.

Education The Centre bridges the gap between the college and the pew by providing top-quality education for Christians in their local churches. This is done through seminars, workshops and conferences.

Research We carry out research into the relationship between Christianity and the modern world. We seek to develop a distinctively Christian voice in response to the critical issues of the day.

Publication The Centre generates a variety of publications, including the C. S. Lewis Centre books published by SPCK, video and audio tapes and occasional papers. We also produce a quarterly journal, *Leading Light*.

For further information, write to: The C. S. Lewis Centre, c/o Dr Andrew Walker, Centre for Educational Studies, King's College London, Cornwall House Annex, Waterloo Road, London SE1 8TX.

PASSION'S PROGRESS

The Meanings of Love

ROGER NEWELL

To Tim

with Love

Roger

First published in Great Britain 1994
Society for Promoting Christian Knowledge
Holy Trinity Church
Marylebone Road
London NW1 4DU

Unless otherwise noted, all scripture references are taken
from The Revised Standard Version of the Bible
© 1971 and 1952.

British Library Cataloguing-in-Publication Data

A catalogue record for this book is available
from the British Library

ISBN 0-281-04757-X

Typeset by Pioneer Associates, Perthshire
Printed in Great Britain by
Redwood Books, Trowbridge, Wiltshire

To
Brian Lake and James Torrance

Contents

Acknowledgements

I am pleased to express my gratitude to the many friends, older and younger, whose companionship, stimulation, and support have encouraged me and made the writing of this book possible. At times I have used portions of their stories and our life together to help in the telling of this story about love. However, out of respect for privacy, these are composites, not exact reproductions.

I particularly wish to express my thanks for the assistance of Jeff Boshears and Ed Eastman in Portland, Andrew Walker of the C. S. Lewis Centre, and the SPCK editorial staff in London, including Judith Longman, Brendan Walsh, and Catherine Mann.

I am profoundly grateful for the support of my family–my parents, Gerald and Catherine Newell, my brother, Clifford S. Newell, who compiled the index, my children, Marilee and Melanie, and the one who shared most intimately in the ups and downs of this task, as in most things, my wife, Sue.

It has been my peculiar blessing to have two mentors as I have inquired into the meaning of love. Though I bear full responsibility for all infelicities of thought or expression presented, and though readers should not identify the ideas expressed herein as synonymous with theirs, nevertheless, without their inspiration and care, this book would not have been written. To them it is gratefully dedicated.

Roger Newell

Introduction

Whenever you start on a journey, it helps to have a map. That way you know more precisely where you are starting and where you are going. Should you get lost while stopping at a pleasing diversion or being a good samaritan for another, a map provides some idea of how to get back on the track. Christian faith provides disciples with a map to the meaning of love in our families, our churches, our communities and nations. It also provides a kind of repair kit to use when things break down.

There are three things I would like to say about this map before you open it to scan or study. First, because love is all about relationships, it is important that the phenomenon of love not be analysed as simply an experience or a list of qualities. Maps have to do with seeing connections. That is, in order to see romantic love clearly, and to experience it fully, it helps to view it in context with other relationships. Therefore this map correlates and connects the numerous love relations, for example, within the self, within the family, within the church community, and between the church and the larger political community, always surrounded by the fundamental relationship of love between God and humankind.

Second, this map charts two journeys of love. The outward journey proceeds from our experience of love as it moves outward from inner conflict to romance, family, church, community, and nation. The return journey explores the beginnings, at once cosmic and personal, of love and its shadow experience, hate. From there the map orientates us through the road-blocks, detours, and developmental processes known as the *via dolorosa*. The final stage of the journey surveyed is love's climactic destiny, and triumph over all that opposes it.

Third, a parable of Kierkegaard helps express how this particular map came to be drawn. Imagine being in a large building, he says, and as you turn a corner, you see two doors with two different signs over the doors. Over one door a sign reads 'heaven'; over the next door the sign reads 'lecture on heaven'. Then you notice that mobs of people are scurrying through the latter door to the lecture. They all bypass the door marked 'heaven'. It is as if some invisible magnet repels them and us from the former, and an unconscious attraction pulls us towards the lecture.

I believe the magnet inhibiting our experience of love (heaven) and making us more comfortable with the lecture is related to what Ian Suttie describes as the 'taboo on tenderness'. This taboo dominates our 'scientific' approach to knowledge about most things, including our knowledge and experience of God and his love. In this taboo, our habits of thought have taught us to mistrust our passions or emotions, and consider them to be of secondary value in connecting us with reality. The very word 'sentimental' is used as a conclusive argument in many discussions, including religious ones. But what if a true knowledge of God involves us in a felt experience of being truly loved? What if I need to discover an appropriate emotional connection, that is, a felt attunement with the reality I seek to know?

Carl Jung once remarked that nowadays people go to the psychiatrist because they no longer *feel* forgiven. Without this felt experience our theological talk is only a peculiar form of intellectual play. Because both emotional and conceptual attunement to reality are vital, this map honours both. It has been drafted along the side of the road, sometimes helping others who are lost, sometimes exploring a pleasing diversion, sometimes when I have been simply broken down or lost, in need of help myself. It is a map exploring the progress of love for those who sense that they themselves are on a journey. After all, if you are only attending a lecture and not on a journey, who needs a map?

PART ONE

1

The Problem of Love

While I was speaking one Sunday morning about the love of God, a group of teenagers was chattering away in the back of the sanctuary, chuckling and having a merry old time. I remember expressing my annoyance, but could not find it in me at that moment to express the love which I was talking about. In view of all the talks on love and the songs on the radio about love I conclude that it is much easier to talk or to sing about love than to be loving. The problem with love is that I am not very good at it. It is hard to love when a barrier or difficulty comes our way, though it is nice to be loved in a painful situation.

Therefore it is tempting out of disappointment or frustration not only to keep quiet about love, but to indulge in a bit of bravado by saying to myself: 'I may not be very loving, but at least I don't pretend to be something I'm not', 'I don't want love, just respect.' Alternatively, one may pursue surrogates such as bodily contact and label that 'love'. But this provides only momentary satisfaction and creates in us addictive patterns of mutually exploitative and temporary relations. Other more pious-appearing substitutes include using the Church to exercise dominance over others and calling that 'deeds of love'. Eventually, to the degree the love has more to do with control than care, the dominating giver is rejected along with their dominating gift.

Love and Criticism

Love and criticism have an awkward coexistence. Hans Selye, the pioneer researcher of the biology of stress, has written that more than any other stressor, criticism and disapproval make our work frustrating and harmful.[1] And yet have you ever noticed how it is easier to criticize your neighbour or co-worker than to love him or her? Have you also noticed that when *you* offer criticism,

3

it seems such a spot-on, incisive comment? But when I receive criticism, I feel misunderstood, superficially assessed by an unsympathetic judge who has missed the main point due to some ulterior motive.

The unacknowledged truth about criticism is that it usually reveals more about the critic than it does about the situation or the person being criticized. Mother comes home from choir practice to find the dishes undone, the children unbathed, and the sitting-room a mess. She responds with a few sharp words towards her 'inconsiderate and disorganized' husband. The criticisms reflect her need for a clean house, her weariness after a long day, and the need to relax, not to wash the children and tidy up before bedtime. Meanwhile the children and dad have done puzzles, board games, played piggy-back, and had a mini-holiday. If interviewed, the children's interpretation of the evening would be rather different: 'Dad is brilliant! He spends time with us rather than reading the paper or doing the chores.' The difference in interpretation (praise or blame) hinges on the fact that mother is left paying the tab for the mini-holiday and her wallet of energy is empty. I wonder what father would have said had he come home late from a hard day's work, tired and hungry, only to find the kitchen disorganized, mum and the children engaged in a glorious baking project, and dinner forgotten?

Once my sense of hurt at being neglected becomes inflamed, it is nearly impossible to think my expectations are inappropriate to the present situation or that a compromise could be possible. Perhaps through long periods of being ignored or forced to conform to others' needs (parents, siblings, partner) it becomes very difficult to consider 'without prejudice' the other person's viewpoint. Far easier to play the blame game, project my dis-ease upon your present behaviour and justify my criticism rather than explore the origins of my expectations in previously unresolved wounds.

There is another way criticism hinders love. These are the times I am not blaming but being blamed. Father loses his temper, shakes his child by the shoulders and shouts, 'You must learn to control yourself', ignoring the fact that he is intent on control-ling the child, and unaware of his own lack of self-control at that very moment. When children or adults receive such criticism they experience guilt, self-hate and deep weariness. There we were, plodding along nicely, intent on such and such a project, when out of nowhere we are stung by an indirect barb which shames us with disapproval, or we are assaulted by an expert in personality dismemberment. 'You selfish thing. Why aren't you . . .' (and they fill in the blank with their needs and preferences at that moment). Inside, we comply: 'Ah, they're right. I'm not a good person. They've seen through me. I'm not very loving.' Full of self-loathing, we feel like failures.

What has happened? I have accepted my critics' verdict as if it were a direct transcript of reality, not a direct expression of their moods and needs. Some of us have learned to take such criticism on the chin, and go down for the count as the best way to survive in a hostile environment. Had we tried to fight back, we would have been in serious jeopardy. Others of us have learned to survive by counter-punching fiercely at the first sign of fault-finding. But the result is an equally discouraging relational mess whether I thump my opponents, or I allow them to pummel me. Sometimes we get stuck in patterns of relating whereby one of us expresses dissatisfaction while the other reacts by not reacting, by barricading himself emotionally and closing in deeper into his shell. Cumulatively, the friendship or marriage is quietly severed. By the time the emotional amputation is recognized, it may be too late to restore, especially if, as is common today, I have secretly re-attached my emotional life to someone else.

The Easy Option

Whether in defence or by attack, criticism seems an easier option than loving my neighbour. It is so attractive because it lets me off the hook. With the everyday magic of fault-finding, the critic wipes his slate clean and excuses himself for his inability to love and to respect the other or simply to embrace the situation and learn from it. 'Thank goodness. It's your fault.' But in an unguarded moment of self-examination I may suspect that I have got it wrong. This is too painful to face for very long, so which of us does not happily return to the 'blame game'? It is easier to confess your sins than to confess mine. I comfort myself by singing the neurotic's national anthem, 'if only'. 'If only you had done . . . x. If only you hadn't done . . . y.' To see the fault lies with you soothes me with the thought, 'If only you were more lovable, I could love you better'. And in a curious symmetry, others find it easy to accept the critical parental voice of their neighbour's assessment as gospel. We gloomily agree,'If only I was more lovable, I would be loved'.

In the full flight of blaming and accusing, we avoid saying: 'If only I was more loving, I could love you better, though it is hard or the waters are choppy.' The blame swallowers, in mid-gulp, never seem to choke and say: 'Half a moment, if you could see my efforts through the eyes of love, you could find words of encouragement rather than dissatisfaction.'

Such patterns repeat themselves with alarming frequency in our lives. Like a cigarette after-taste, an aroma of guilt lingers inside of me because I know I ought to be a caring person even when it is not easy. I ought to love. It is good to love. I try. I fail. It is my fault. I withdraw in pain, lick my wounds by despising myself, or by blaming my failures on the poor materials I am stuck with. I criticize or I swallow criticism whole. I play the 'if only' game. But underneath, when I am the blamer, I feel anxious because I sense this blocked relationship reflects rather badly on me. Or when I am the 'blamee' I not only accept at face value the accusations others toss my way, but proceed to heap shovels of blame on myself. For the 'blamee' guilt feelings are not an after-taste, but the main course. As a 'blamee', I become worn down and depressed. I am so weary from fending off the accusations of others or of myself, I have no energy left for any creative tasks. These role patterns often take on an institutional life of their own in parent-child and employer-employee relationships. That is the problem of love. How do I break out of this system of failure, guilt, and larding blame on others or upon myself?

Missing Pieces of the Puzzle–Respect

For love to endure in a situation of mounting pressure to blame, counter-blame, or simply to walk out, a new component in the relational system needs to be integrated: respect, which literally means 'to see again'. When I review or reflect I take time to 'look again' at the person I am in conflict with, not as I want them to be, pleased or praising, but as they are, taking them seriously on their terms, not according to my needs and preferences. With the gift of 'seeing again' on new terms, my burden to defend, counter-attack, or solve my critic's concerns, is lightened.

Criticism, subtle or blunt, reveals that an inner energy field of needs and expectations within my critic, and only indirectly related to me, have been aroused. In pain, the critic projects this internal situation (effect) outwardly upon me (the cause). With self-respect I look again and no longer willy-nilly accept the criticism as an objective pronouncement. With respect for my critics, I look again at his words and see them as expressing his unresolved concerns, and I do not inflatedly assume that I hold the key to, let alone understand the problem. It is more possible to love my neighbour, and not to feel defensive or downright wretched about my failures when I no longer assume that my critics are giving objective descriptions of my behaviour or worth, but are making statements from their inner distress. When a parent, colleague or spouse has an inner wound which they believe my behaviour has activated, it is patronizing to humbly assume that the degree of their distress is primarily my creation. I may be the last straw, but I am not the haystack, and the sharp edge of their tongue may have been well grounded by previous whetstones before acquiring its current edge.

There is no progress in love for me or my critic either to simply allow the criticism to run its penetrating course or to counter-attack in kind. It is more helpful to respect and to explore the powerful personal origins of our urge to point out the shortcomings of others and our, equally, strong reactions to criticism, rather than anxiously try to attack, defend, or 'fix-it'. The child may feel quite loved after the mini-holiday, but for the wife the whole scene may have reactivated a lifetime of feeling left to clear up after the pleasures of others. Certainly the care given to the children stands as a positive experience. But player and payer for the holiday need to re-negotiate who pays the tab.

Loving Our Enemies–Within and Without

In our modern era, depth psychology suggests a further key to unlock the closed system of failure and blaming. It says: 'Do you know what the problem is? You cannot love others until you love yourself. You cannot love yourself because you have been the recipient of well-meaning, but fault-finding parental voices ever since you were born. Hence your feeling of being loved and your ability to love has been based on performance. You only felt loved and accepted when you smiled at the right time, said the right word, obeyed. You tried like heaven to please because it felt so comforting to be caressed with smiles and hugs for good behaviour. But you received them only when you performed correctly. When you were not nice or clever, you received nothing, except a rebuke. Hence the reason you find it so hard to love your neighbour when she is neither nice nor clever, and are unable to stop criticizing or internalizing criticism to the quick from your neighbour (employer, spouse and so on), is because you are unable to love yourself. You are disappointed and possibly quite angry at yourself. You had goals and dreams and you feel you have let yourself down rather badly.' The Swiss psychologist Carl Jung put this in a most compelling way:

> The acceptance of oneself is the essence of the moral problem and the epitome of a whole outlook upon life. That I feed the hungry, that I forgive an insult, that I love my enemy in the name of Christ—all these are undoubtedly great virtues. What I do unto the least of my brethren, that I do unto Christ. But what if I should discover that the least among them all, the poorest of all the beggars, the most impudent of all the offenders, the very enemy himself—that these are within me, and that I myself stand in need of the alms of my own kindness—that I myself am the enemy who must be loved—what then?[2]

Here is the missing puzzle piece that depth psychology provides: it is as we accept and love ourselves as we are, warts and all, that we can learn to love others when they do not measure well against our standards. I can love like this because I have learned to accept and forgive myself when I do not perform to my expectations.

Bitter-sweet is the breakthrough which reveals the reason we are too frequently critical of others: our criticisms are coded statements about ourselves. It explains volumes. No wonder when I have tried to 'help' or 'love' or 'give advice' you have not seemed to appreciate it. It is because my 'love' was for an ideal you that I am searching for, who will give me the support and care I have yet to find. This is who I love and hunger for. This is who I wish you would be for me. I do not actually love the real you and you know it. I cannot give you an acceptance and love which I have yet to receive and feel within myself, which I do not feel about myself. Instead I spread via my 'love' the pain and fault-finding of my own self-disapproval and disappointment. Keith Miller has written:

I realized why I point out others' mistakes and omissions . . . I now see that I tell them about their mistakes as a way of controlling them, bolstering my own weak self-esteem and suppressing my fear of not being adequate. After all, if they make lots of mistakes, I'll look better—less likely to be judged inadequate by comparison.[3]

Jung, Miller, and others have indeed recovered a long neglected clue to the problem of love. When Jesus says love your neighbour as yourself, he implies it is of equal importance to love yourself as it is to love your neighbour. In fact, the road to loving my neighbour may begin by loving and forgiving myself in a deeper way. Until I do this, my capacity to care for my neighbour will be rather shallow, though perhaps a bit noisy (1 Cor. 13.1). But this clue leads us into an even more critical problem of love.

The Intervention

Modern psychology tells me I need to love and respect myself if I would truly love others. At first this sounds hopeful, but what if I honestly do not like my emotions, my appearance or my behaviour? Self-hate is particularly acute in young people. We often single out the youth for being narcissistic in the sense of being in love only with self, and many obediently feel guilty. But what if a closer look at this life-style of self-absorption suggests a rather strong self-dislike? Bruce Springsteen, one of the premier rock singers and writers, describes the youthful self-contempt: 'I check my look in the mirror, I wanna change my clothes, my hair, my face, Man, I ain't getting nowhere.' As a result, the young rush to identify with someone else–a pop group, a successful athlete–or try to imitate someone else in order to escape relentless self and parental disapproval. There are a myriad destructive ways to escape as well. Had they felt loved and accepted, they would not endure the torture of continually trying to win approval alternately by being different or by being like everyone else.

If only I could love myself. I ought to love myself. I can only love other people if I genuinely love and accept myself and stop projecting my self-dislike onto others. But how do I love and accept what is unacceptable? Can you see how the missing clue of self-love easily becomes another great principle which judges me as a failure? One may feel even more miserable than ever for not loving one's self as one ought. Left in isolation, unrelated to a greater truth about love, the new insights of psychology, like religions of rule and achievement before it, drop us deeper into the descending spiral of failure in loving and accelerate our sense of guilt and discouragement. The psychologist becomes the latest and loudest critical parental voice from which I try to win love by my good behaviour and my earnest acceptance of his ideals and theories.

What help does the Bible offer? Some think its help consists in giving us a divine set of standards to help us more tightly monitor our behaviour and heighten our spiritual quality control through the Ten Commandments and the Sermon on the Mount. Unfortunately, increasing our knowledge of right and wrong does not solve the problem. King David knew it was wrong to commit adultery with Bathsheba and murder Uriah, her husband. The problem is greater.

The biblical message is more than good advice about what we ought to do. It reveals a reality which interrupts this cycle of criticism and guilt for the 'oughts' to which we never measure up. The first letter of John puts it this way: 'In this is love, not that we loved God but that he loved us and sent his Son to be the atonement for our sins . . . We love, because he first loved us' (1 John 4.11,19). According to the Bible, our crisis in loving is so radical that the sheer reality of God must enter into our situation and accompany us within the problem of love. Here are no fresh demands: Love yourself! Love your neighbour! Change yourself! Accept yourself! Here is God entering our broken humanity, loving us and converting us as Immanuel, *God with us*, within the awkward particularities of living.

Why believe God really loves me like this? Perhaps my parents' love was attached by one too many strings to feel confident that I was worthy of love or truly valued. Why believe that God loves the real me behind my persona of kindness and competence which masks my fears, weakness and pride? Doesn't God only truly love me if I repent and am a good, loving person? It is undeniable that the Church has implied this many times, that God only loves the truly good, loving heart. The well-known devotional classic, *The Imitation of Christ,* says: 'If thou couldst empty thyself perfectly of all created things, Jesus would willingly dwell with thee.'[4] But what if I have not truly emptied myself, have not truly loved as I ought? What if I have tried and failed repeatedly? What if I am sick of trying? We are back to the crux of the problem. I ought to love, and I have failed. I ought to confess my sins and I do a poor job of it. It is never good enough! What if, like the young prodigal, I have escaped from all my family obligations only to find myself isolated and afraid, considering a new reform package as a last ditch bargain? What if, like the elder brother, I have been a model citizen, but my damaged relationships with father and younger brother are so full of hurt and resentment they reveal a connection to the Father which is more physical than personal?

My answer is the New Testament's answer: Jesus Christ comes alongside us in mercy and judgement to take our judgement upon himself, to interrupt our habit of playing God by assessing and judging ourselves and others. The cross is nothing less than the coming of God in Jesus, stretching his arms wide to bear our sins, forgive our pride, and create a new basis for our relationships. He exchanges the old ways with a new foundation: not the earning of credits and the establishing of league tables, but the freedom and cleansing of living from grace. Christianity is not a new demand to love or to be lovable; it is God coming in human flesh enabling and discipling me into becoming a lover myself.

No one has put it better than George Herbert:

Love bade me welcome: yet my soul drew back,
      Guiltie of dust and sinne.
But quick-ey'd Love, observing me grow slack
      From my first entrance in,
Drew nearer to me, sweetly questioning,
      If I lack'd any thing.

A guest, I answer'd, worthy to be here:
      Love said, You shall be he.
I, the unkinde, ungratefull? Ah my deare,
      I cannot look on thee.
Love took my hand, and smiling did reply,
      Who made the eyes but I?

Truth Lord, but I have marr'd them: let my shame
      Go where it doth deserve.
And know you not, sayes Love, who bore the blame?
      My deare, then I will serve.
You must sit down, sayes Love, and taste my meat:
      So I did sit and eat.

A New World Destabilizing and Re-interpreting the Old

Love is often more of a problem than a pleasure, a code word for control rather than care. Self-love is a helpful servant, but a harsh master. But in the world of the Bible love is a gift, not a reward, for it is centred in Jesus Christ. Soon a contemporary pilgrim makes one further unwelcome discovery as he proceeds towards the celestial city: the pilgrim's path between blaming and being blamed seems more non-existent than narrow. It is as if I am locked in a wrestling match in which either I am on top but threatened and must press my advantage to stay in control, or I am on the defensive, struggling with my feelings of failure, resenting my critic-accuser, counter-punching furiously, or walking out of relationships. How can God's love take root and grow within such hostile soil?

It helps to step back and assess the situation away from the intensity of the combative climate. This atmosphere of combat characterizes the problem of love as a very competitive fight in which one is on top, struggling for dominance, the other squirms on the bottom, weak and pressured to submit. What binds the blamer and blamee together is this strange dance of striving for superiority and resisting of inferiority. I believe the clue to interpreting the meaning of this deadly pattern is the recognition that we are in fact engaged in the ancient and fundamentally competitive warfare which is pride, whether I am struggling from below (inferiority) or struggling to maintain control from the top (superiority). As victim or victimizer, we are caught in the spider's web of pride, which C. S. Lewis has called the great sin, defining it as essentially competitive.[5]

How do I feel when I live locked in pride's competitive struggle? Consider one of the basic pleasures which a lover can give or receive: a smile. When I am living in pride's competitive frame of mind, I do not so much enjoy my child's smile as I am driven to evaluate it, or possess it: 'Her smile is more pretty than that of other children', 'Her smile is not quite as nice as my neighbour's down the road.' Both over-valuing or under-valuing only make sense within a competitive mental system. I do not really enjoy the gift of that smile; I use it to prop up or damage my self-esteem and worth over against someone else. The same process occurs with my child's painting, her homework, her mother's work, my own work. Is it better or worse than x's or y's? By contrast, love creates a non-competitive world of contemplation and celebration. When I receive another's smile, I am able to focus with immediacy and enjoy its affection, beauty and companionship. I let it roll over my senses and embrace me, without needing to assign it a mark.

Perhaps we are pursuing knowledge and we disagree or are unequal in our experience and skill, as with tutor and student. If the atmosphere is free of envy and rivalry, we may together freely explore our differences without feeling the need to come out on top, or 'hold our own'. But when my analysis and criticism do not spring from enjoyment and receptivity, I signal that to be loved you must earn approval over against rivals for my affection.

Let us return to the smile. What happens when I cease competing? I return in gratitude to the smile I've been granted, but have taken for granted. I enjoy the smile. I receive the painting in an evaluation-free, receptive state of mind and heart. Having first received and enjoyed my daughter's painting, my response or feedback will not pass on pride's competitive atmosphere, be it inflated or deflated, for example, 'Did you win a high mark?', but will encourage in both of us a closer study of what makes trees so delightful to view and what magic it is I may capture with paints to pass this delight onto paper or canvas.

When I am competing in the 'who has the prettiest or most clever child' sweepstakes, I am using a smile or a talent or any other gift from God's good creation as a means of expressing or expanding my power, status and superiority. I use the gift for power over you. Hence I enjoy neither the gift nor you because I am using the one to have power over the other. This irreducibly competitive element is the spiritual cancer which eats up the very possibility of love. Meanwhile, the gift cries out not to be compared but enjoyed and delighted in as beautiful and good in and of itself.

Love's Alternative to Competitive Criticism

Every teacher knows that skills and talents must be valued and given opportunity for further development in order that they may reach their true fulfilment. As surely as competitive criticism discourages development, studies reveal the importance of corrective feedback so that behaviour is not frustrated, stagnant and censured but guided more closely to its goal. How can this occur without disapproving criticism, the great stressor? Love's

alternative is a co-operative, unconditionally supportive framework. It may be most appropriate and even urgent for a partner,
colleague or employer to give corrective feedback, but it is
supportive and strengthens development only within a framework of mutuality, lest we communicate to a colleague or fellow
pilgrim that we are sizing them up or grading them, within the
atmosphere of superiority and inferiority, and imply 'this is not
quite as good as x and y. You are less valuable than z'.

In the old world of pride I compete with my neighbour for
superiority. There is no room for enjoyment and love, only
victory and defeat. Love interrupts pride's strangling interaction
when in the face of comparing and competing, I name my dis-ease
and allow my fear of defeat and my wish-dream of conquest to
be put to death, so I may encounter my neighbour in a new
arena. I experience the smile of my child in the singularity of one
person's affectionate movement towards another, as an unrepeatable work of spiritual art which in one frozen moment captures a
movement of joy and freedom in that hinge of space and time.
Of course the smile must grow in sincerity and depth of respect
and love, lest it becomes bent into a tool for manipulation and is
used to control others. All of this development awaits a smile
through interaction with the neighbour's response. But it reaches
maturity as parents and friends respond within a context of
receptivity and enjoyment, not evaluative comparison.

Competing for Love

Now it must eventually be openly admitted that I am naming and
challenging a great cultural inhibitor of love. The fact is that
Western culture often describes and envisions the fundamental
freedoms and values of its life within a framework of competition. Clearly within proper boundaries a system of economic
competition enhances consumer choice and the availability of
products. It even increases reward for certain skills and labour.
But without clear boundaries and over-arching values of love,
worth, and respect, our so-called free markets quickly degenerate
into a most primitive kind of social Darwinism with tragic consequences for maturity and growth in human relationships, denying
or ignoring all that Jesus has taught us in regards to the centrality of love. When personal relationships are interpreted and
experienced within a competitive arena, loving and being loved

are infected with pride's toxins of superiority and inferiority. With my siblings, partner, and neighbour, envy arises as I wrestle fiercely for my share of recognition and worth. In a competitive framework, more for me means less for you. 'Her smile is lovely' means essentially 'lovelier than yours'. 'My job is valuable' means 'in comparison with yours'.

To analyse the social structures within which love is experienced means that love relationships have social, and no doubt environmental, consequences. Just as significantly, social conditions profoundly influence our 'habits of the heart', particularly our capacity to give and to receive love. Within a predatory social and economic structure of the survival and success of the (self-proclaimed) fittest, love relationships based on mutual respect and unconditional worth will be limited to a mutant strain in society which has carefully qualified and put interior boundaries around the competitive mentality. Similarly problematic is the structure of a hierarchical or feudal system of relations based on hereditary privilege and the ownership of property. Such a system leads to controlled and rather rigidly demarcated relations of dominance and submission.

This feudal pattern of dominance and submission still filters down whenever our notions of respect for tradition and authority imply that it is wrong to ask questions or express doubts regarding the received way of applying certain traditions in the present. Religion is the obvious example of how the received tradition of doctrine or practice becomes almost identical to the reality of God in his innermost being. But the same anxious identification and call to submit is at work elsewhere. Max Planck's scientific autobiography documents how his new ideas were seen as deviation from the received scientific textbooks of his era and only became working hypotheses upon the retirement and deaths of the leading teachers and editors of that generation.[6] In psychology the maturity of that new science was seriously restricted by the formation of a Freudian orthodoxy with a committee installed to monitor uniformity, with the ostracism of those who dared to question basic assumptions or experiment with different therapeutic techniques. In politics we have only to look at the Marxist purges in Eastern Europe or the McCarthy trials in America to see how a group attachment to a political outlook can become highly anxious and heavily defended against questioning, reformulation and reformation.

Of course, in the presence of highly restrictive and controlling systems, and the absence of mutually respectful and egalitarian relationships, substitutes for love will emerge. Neighbours, partners, and peers will be used, not enjoyed, on a temporary, pragmatic basis, as commodities for the extraction of pleasure or status. Colleagues and congregations become numerical reinforcements for an emotional safety net provided by group consensus to a set of beliefs. But when I use others, they are not received as persons to be enjoyed, as valuable and intrinsically worthy in and for themselves alone.

It would be unfair to suggest that pride's predatory struggle for superiority is unique to the 'free' market culture of the West. As long as Marxism undergirded socialism and demonized any form of market economy, its use of the class struggle model to interpret the meaning of life and history advocated and enshrined as dogma the necessity of 'class warfare' and the use of force to dominate and control its opponents. In whatever system, left or right, an infrastructure of dominance and submission creates the familiar clash whereby pride competes and love structurally suffocates. There seems to be no alternative but for the Christian vision of a kingdom of love to explore a path beyond these two competing and competitive systems in order to build a nurturing structural environment for love to grow. Consider these facts: the Marxist dinosaur in the East has toppled; the largest capitalist nation in the West has an almost unimaginable debtor status and is approaching bankruptcy; and the poverty of weaker debtor nations increases under intolerable foreign debt contracted under their former military dictatorships. Is not the urgent challenge for the next generation of economists and politicians to create structures which are inspired by the central Christian conviction that love, mutuality, and equal worth cry out for co-operative structures in order for humanity to flourish, not rigid traditionalist ones of dominance and submission, nor the recently revived but nonetheless reptilian system based on unregulated predatory competition?

Love's Distribution System

There is another facet to pride's competitive distortion of our ability to give and receive love. I have in mind here the 'wounded awareness' that because love occurs in a competitive world of power, there is an unfair distribution of resources and skills. Whereas some appear, from the outside, to breeze through problems in love as in life, others seem to progress only through intense struggle and even then show only fragile progress for all the travail and pain. Since we are at such a competitive advantage or disadvantage over against each other, how can God truly love us equally? How can God love the ethically mature and the moral midget both the same? Within the competitive model, such a belief is nonsense. But God's love toils in a proud world with a humble heart. God loves a sinner equally to a saint because our personal maturity and talents are not the defining features of our humanity, nor the magnets which compel God's attention and care. Some may have more artistic talent, some more potential for spiritual sensitivity. But God loves us not for our personal talents or attractive potential, but because he is unprovoked love. God is not in competition within himself. He abides in the harmony of enjoying and being enjoyed, in the rhythm of emptying and being filled. His love experiences no competitive threat nor a shortage of supply for God is within himself a completed enjoyment only hinted at in our hymnody: 'Wild and sweet' . . . 'a love like a river, a fountain, an ocean' . . . 'fairer, purer than all the angels heaven can boast.' Love's perfection celebrates a mutuality of trust and courage. It is the farthest distance from comparing smiles, assigning a mark, and preferring the prettier. God delights in the sheer unnecessary surprise and wrinkled creases of each. And if the Psalms are any clue, he does not despise our frowns or tears.

When God wore our human flesh in Jesus, was Jesus physically superior in strength to Samson or intellectually equipped with more grey matter than Einstein? Did various personal qualities give him a competitive edge in being fully loved by the Father? We can be confident that Jesus's victory has nothing to do with this. If value and love from God is so earned then Jesus too stands well down the list.

What distinguishes Jesus in relation to the Father is the perfect mutuality of loving and being loved in the Spirit's glad rhythm and his sheer trust in his Father's faithfulness. From the beginning, and so for us, God's love is not achieved at the expense of a rival nor forced out of the Divine as a concession to our talents and spiritual attractiveness. It is being embraced, trusted, and valued in a covenant of mercy and judgement.

God's love does not create winners and losers. Such identities are only brewed within pride's competitive cauldron. Elder brother, prodigal, thief on the cross, John the beloved disciple, the poor, lame, harlots, and outcasts are all invited to the same banquet with patriarchs and prophets. While all of us were far away, the Father saw us and came running.

Yes, it does appear at times that some have an easy passage, whereas others struggle for every inch of progress. Certainly we are in danger of a competitive, envious assessment here. Fairness is an issue which will not go away and we must openly admit that some of us chose our parents and cultures (and sub-cultures) better than others did. In such a mood of awareness one may look at a saint and resent his support: 'Saul of Tarsus may have been a rogue, but he was granted a vision I would give anything to receive!' Of course, St Paul's vision led him to anything but an easy passage. To whom much is given, much is demanded. St Paul travelled a path full of grace and mercy, to be sure. But for him it meant that God's love was known in shipwrecks, imprisonment, and eventual martyrdom. Jesus himself, the Lord of love, was made perfect (presumably in love) through what he suffered (Heb. 5.8). When in Luke's gospel we read that Jesus grew in stature and in favour with God and man, the word 'grow' takes its meaning from a nautical image, whereby one beats one's way forward blow by blow, as in rowing. His love was climactically released and known in the events of Good Friday, preparing him and us for the celebration and vindication of Easter. The servant is not greater than the master. Some may breeze through life. No one breezes into mature love. There is a cross in the way for each of us which is non-negotiable.

Cross-shaped love always surprises and interrupts our ideals and expectations. The utterly real journey of God's love in Jesus touches our disappointment in our failed ideal of ourselves, others, and our inflated, or deflated, estimation of our achievements. In other words, God's love deconstructs our competitive prison of pride's inferiority/superiority belligerence in order to reconstruct these from a new foundation. This fresh start is what Jesus likens to new birth. The New Testament writers went so far as to remint an obscure Greek word to convey their discovery that God loves the way Jesus loves. The word they baptized into this discovery was a little-used word, *agape*. Ever since then, the reality behind the word continues to intervene, reinterpret, and rebuild lives worn down by the 'if onlys', 'ought tos', and competitive warfare.

Suppose the next time mother comes in from choir practice, father has once again in his dilatory playfulness neglected to tidy or prepare the children for bed. Her response is: 'Well, it looks as if everyone's been having a good time.' The husband, gratified for the measured calm of his weary wife's words, gently but firmly summons the children to go upstairs and jump in the bath, while he tidies up and mother sits down and has five minutes' peace and a cup of tea. Following tea, bath and teeth-brushing, mother and father will jointly tuck the children into bed. The children, remembering the recent confrontation and sensing a new approach, rush upstairs, pleased to contribute towards a more equitable arrangement of play and responsibility tonight.

As I kneel to pray for my critic in the presence of agape, I no longer see simply an enemy, his sword outstretched, seeking to hurt me. I see a wounded brother in pain, himself in a world of warriors competing for limited quantities of recognition and care, locked in mortal combat for diminishing supplies of affection and love. In the new climate released by this recognition, my efforts at loving, weary from the interruptions of both critics and criticizing, are in this present moment being reinterpreted and re-experienced. Redeemed. The old problems reappear in new guises of course. The criticism, whether intended competitively or co-operatively, is by grace, re-experienced as feedback, helping me to correct my path and to interpret more appropriately my brother's indirect expression of pain. My own deeds of love are known in their proper modesty and realism, with a less inflated evaluation of their potential achievement. And in a non-competitive climate where criticism is self-initiated, we are grateful for the feedback and mutual problem-solving which keeps us from wasting time or 'missing the mark' (the primary meaning of the most common Greek word for 'sin'), helping us clarify our goals and correct our progress.

In jarring opposition, critic and recipient are torn apart into combat zones of attack, counter-attack, and withdrawal. The realism of agape reconnects these sheer opposites through the crucifixion of our ego's proud warfare with our adversary. But as we shall see, just as urgent as the confrontation with our critics is agape's encounter with our lovers.

Notes

1 Hans Selye, *Stress Without Distress*, (Signet, 1975), p. 99.
2 Carl Jung, *Modern Man in Search of a Soul*, (Harvest, 1933), p. 235.
3 J. Keith Miller, *Compelled to Control*, (Health Communications, 1992), p. 137.
4 Thomas À Kempis, *The Imitation of Christ*, 3.5.
5 C. S. Lewis, *Mere Christianity*, (Macmillan, 1977), p. 109.
6 cf. Max Planck, *Scientific Autobiography and Other Papers*, (Williams and Norgate Limited, 1950).

2

Romantic Love

When we hear the word 'love' today, the first kind we think of is usually romantic love. Romantic love is the kind we fall 'in' and 'out of'. It is the kind singers sing about, or wail about when it is gone. When we are in love, we cannot say anything good enough about life. When we have fallen out of love, or our partner's love for us has grown cold, we cannot say anything bad enough. Romantic love is great while it lasts, but too often it does not last long. Why is this?

I believe it is because romantic love begins as an image, a paper doll cut-out I have in my mind of the perfect partner for me. This inner paper doll is an ideal I soak up from my culture which has many sources: conversations with parents and peers, novels I have read, and the countless movies, television dramas, or advertisements which have massaged my mind. I pin this doll onto you. If you will wear it, then I am in love. I love you because I desire that image and you fulfil and fit my image. But as I get to know the real you, your peculiarities, dare I say faults, make it increasingly difficult to desire and idealize you. You keep changing and moving and messing up the paper doll I have stuck on you. We have fallen out of love as surely as once we fell in. That is when a crisis arises. It would be nice and tidy if this falling in and out business ceased once the decision to marry has been reached. But the alarming fact is that once there are no more hindrances and my ideal is attained and actual, not a dream, something near the heart of the passion dies. It is as if obstacles and impossibilities fed the passion and their elimination eliminates the oxygen which fuels passion's fires.

I may of course continue to love my ideal woman, my paper doll, and stick my fantasy onto any number of people, falling in and out of love any number of times, leaving the discarded persons behind as so many disposable manikins. Or I may lay my paper doll cut-out to one side and learn to love the flesh and blood woman which real life has put into my arms. Such a person is not half-goddess, half-dream, but a real person, with faults and frailties rather like me. If I relentlessly seek romantic love, I may forever find it, albeit in a fleeting chain of multiple relationships, but I will not find a lasting, maturing love relationship.

One frequently comes across some writer or speaker who tries to give reality to, or at least work out, a compromise with our paper doll and the lecture may be titled 'How to keep the romance alive in your marriage', but the series of techniques about how to dress, what to say, what not to say, only prolongs the 'paper doll' stage of life and frustrates the real person wanting to be loved. Better to withdraw the idealization altogether and learn to adjust caringly to the imperfect sinner alongside me, who I will romantically desire . . . occasionally, not absolutely and utterly, as one would some goddess in a drama.

The Religion of Passion

Perhaps we can now better understand why the New Testament writers, when describing God's love, deliberately avoided the most celebrated word for love in the Greek language, *eros*. From this word we have derived a whole family of words describing the longing and desire which we particularly associate with romantic attraction. The word they chose instead, agape, describes the quality of God's love which redeems this fickle side of eros, which enables me to reconsider my fascination for my 'paper doll' ideal. After all, are not my partner's needs and goals and struggles as important as my own? What about her 'paper doll' image which I have shattered?

The Bible nowhere rejects or denigrates eros. From the Genesis account of Adam's attraction for Eve, which remedies his loneliness with a suitable partner ('At last here is bone of my bones, and flesh of my flesh') to the soaring celebration of physical intimacy in the Song of Solomon ('Let him kiss me with the kisses of his mouth–for your love is better than wine'), it honours eros as a precious gift which expresses an aspect of God's own character as the one who is the husband of the Church and who prepares for his beloved a wedding feast. It refuses, however, to make the erotic experience of sweet desire the primary feature of love for God or love for others. Where we do make eros central, we experience the crisis of exalting a good gift into a god, and inadvertently creating a demonic force by our idolatry.

Let us be quite clear that we are descending from the dominant winds of western popular culture which idealize the experience of ecstatic longing. We are doubting the culture-wide belief that happiness shall flee should we be forced to land in the rather homely forms of religion below us in the mundane neighbourhoods, churches, and dwellings down the road. In a society with a strongly materialistic atmosphere and assumptions, the remnants of mystical experience are borne on the wings of the restless quest for romantic fulfilment. We are in fact confronting the unofficial religion of every man: the promise of true and lasting happiness if only romantic and sexual fulfilment can be found. This religion presents its 'worship experience' in the countless movable temples of best-seller novels, block-buster movies, and popular music. So pervasively popular and unquestioned is the mystical religion of romantic love that most businesses and marketing advertisements, knowing they are tapping into a highly energized circuit, use the mere suggestion of romance to sell us almost anything, from cars to chocolate bars.

Even the greatest religious theme, sacrifice, animates the romantic vows of love. One is willing to surrender anything–a throne, a job, a family, security–for the sake of romantic longing: 'I won't regret what I did for love . . . I would give anything for you . . . You are the air that I breathe . . . I can't live without you. . . .' Descriptions repeating this theme are never-ending. Passion's preference for death to life without the desired is repeated fiercely and frequently from the ancient celtic myth of Tristan and Iseult to Shakespeare's *Romeo and Juliet*, and now with their modern imitators. The only thing one cannot sacrifice is the passionate state of 'being in love' itself. Neglected is the fact that unending sacrifices to this exalted state of desire have enormous potential for cruel and destructive consequences to one's actual friends and family and community who may be sacrificed for romantic exultation and the god or goddess who, temporarily, arouses it. For as every reader of Greek mythology recalls, the deities on Mount Olympus seem never actually to live in anything approaching domestic peace, but are ever and again desiring, abandoning, quarrelling, being jealous, and compulsively repeating the erotic process.

When something promises ultimate value and reward, and is so successfully and frequently used to sell chocolates and cars, and frequently causes such personal tragedy, there is an unmistakable odour of decay in the air. This lofty drama of romantic bliss easily descends to the anxious hunger for sexual stimulation. Tristan's one great sacrifice for Iseult degenerates into Don Juan's countless pursuit of one passion after another. The idealized goddess, the Helen of Troy who nations fight over, becomes an object of pleasure to use and discard in the service of passion. Today most love songs and stories are little more than shallow 'blue suede shoes' songs of exhilaration with the depth of 'tutti-frutti'. These 'fast-food' expressions of romantic love reflect the unromantic fact that without a greater love, mere romance fails so frequently that one in three marriages ends in divorce in the United Kingdom. The one-in-two divorce rate in the USA reveals that the romantic chapel's back door leads to a slaughterhouse of dismembered partners. Nor are second marriages statistically more successful. Uninterpreted by and unintegrated within a profounder reality of love, a consuming passion for romance paradoxically renders romantic love unsustainable. The social and psychological consequences caused by this systemic marital breakdown are so disturbing that presently we are in a state of avoidance lest we despair. And it is worth remembering that in 1993 in Britain alone, the 'fruit' of such passion was that one in four pregnancies was terminated in abortion.

Sexual Passion

Falling in love usually includes a strong element of sexual desire. Though sexual activity prior to marriage is exceedingly common, there seems little evidence that it does anything other than exacerbate the fickleness and short-lived nature of romantic love. Why is this? I suspect it is because rather than reflecting maturity, sexual experimentation is proportional to deprivations and difficulties in our previous and current emotional attachments. Sex takes the form of an outer substitute for inner emotional bonding and often reflects a discouraged, even desperate, search for intimacy among those who lack the maturity and skills to achieve it. When *Psychology Today* interviewed 357 people, asking why they had remained married, the issue of sex was only listed thirteenth for men and fifteenth for women. The first four reasons for remaining married were the same for both sexes: they liked each other, were best friends, valued the lifelong commitment, and the sanctity of the promises.[1]

Consider our children who are beginning to explore friendship with the opposite sex. By the time of adolescence, they have already been the subjects of the vast panoply of media; Hollywood, business sales and saturation marketing, proclaiming the gospel of romantic experience. In the United States it is estimated that the average television viewer sees 20,000 scenes suggesting sexual intercourse each year.[2] Is it surprising that America has the highest teenage pregnancy rate of any developed country? What reasons shall we give to encourage them to doubt the essential devotional ritual of sexual intimacy preceding marriage? With the spread of life-threatening diseases, the argument of physical safety may seem self-evident. But such is the passionate piety of the romantic culture that mere safety seems insipid common sense to one within the sacred realm of passion. Smoking is also harmful to health, but cigarette sales show no sign of decreasing among the young. The romance of smoking–the images of independence from parental control, toughness, daring despite the dangers–merely add to the appeal. The pleasant and repetitive oral and tactile stimulation adds further reinforcement. Sexual experience advertises the great escape from all that is dull and mundane, into an exalted state of pleasure and passion. When one is a true believer in passion, passion must be obeyed. When our sexuality is emotionally identified with the grand drama of romantic fulfilment, safety seems either another obstacle in the quest for true passionate experience which one must risk, or else a pedantic inconvenience compared with the primacy of passion. Besides, passion is fuelled by obstacles.

There is the further problem that being prematurely bonded in a physical way makes it nearly impossible to become intimately acquainted with the other as a person. As interest in one another as stimulating companions begins to diminish, and to avoid the grief of separation, attempts to coerce intimacy through physical closeness arise. Sometimes the very 'urge to merge' increases as the personal relationship is floundering. With the threat of boredom, physical involvement urgently compensates for a fading dream of personal rapport. The very strength of the sexual attachment blocks further opportunity to develop emotional intimacy and to explore whether there is a genuine mutual interest, respect and shared outlook on other aspects of life. Each becomes a substitute comfort figure, a sexual teddy bear for the other, a 'part-object'.

The secret of eros is that it always remains true to itself, not to persons. Passion's promise is faithfulness to its own relentless desire. For a period of time, the person and the passion overlap. When the euphoric idealization ends in an unideal landing, and the 'person' is finally glimpsed, we discover that what we made love to was our 'paper doll' ideal projected onto a partner who is quite distinct from and perhaps far apart from our own values and preferences. At first we may be so eager to wear someone's ideal image and be so admired, we do not have or know or care enough about our own values, beliefs and preferences. We eagerly wish to be the most important person in the world for just one other person, to be adored, and treasured. We wish to crown our life with an adoring, devoted admirer, who continually is delighted by our mere presence.

It is a humbling fact that most marriages begin in a rhapsodic egotism of undigested passion. Nonetheless our passions can progress. Emotional maturity can indeed develop and hence physical intimacy can become a lasting not a fleeting experience. Our very 'fall' into such a marriage may become the womb which expands and contracts to give birth to a mature interdependent adult partnership. But premature sexual activity reveals a tendency to postpone sacrifice, mutual adaptation and transformation. Exposed is our deep hunger for gratification, pleasure, and stimulation; our preference for being in love with love, not a real human person who is sometimes lovely, sometimes not. But for a relationship to deepen, sacrifice and transformation cannot be avoided. The longer we wait and the more habits of postponement we weave around us, the harder progress becomes.

God's Love: Giving not Receiving?

How can God's love both relativize and revitalize romantic love? If the heart of divine love is not this hungering desire, what does the Bible describe as the core ingredient of love? Many writers, following Nygren, describe agape as consisting in 'sacrifice and self-giving', and having nothing to do with 'acquisitive desire'.[3]

Agape is self-giving. It is caring instead of being cared for. It is self-sacrifice without thought of reward. There is surely something that rings true here. But I cannot help thinking this picture derives from a reaction to the exaltation of eros and the using of another person as mere fuel so my passion may continue to burn. In repulsion, we choose a compensating negative ethic of duty. But this is a pale picture of love, as if it consists in self-denial and self-sacrifice and as if longing, reward and pleasure have no place in God's love for creation or our love for God. 'Indeed', as C. S. Lewis puts it, 'if we consider the unblushing promises of reward and the staggering nature of the rewards promised in the Gospels, it would seem that Our Lord finds our desires, not too strong, but too weak.'[4]

When we define giving as the centre of agape, we ignore the fact that much giving is contaminated by greed or possessiveness even as much receiving is grabbing. The mother who is always doing things for her children, not for their sakes, but in order to keep them dependent in order to ward off her own loneliness, is giving in the wrong sort of way. Taking care of someone can be a very selfish business indeed. I need to help you too much, not for your sake, but for my sake. I serve for all the wrong reasons: to earn approval, in competitive rivalry, to be at centre stage, to have you indebted to me, and so on. One wonders if more cruelty has not been done by those desperate to give than those desperate to take. At least it has been more insidious for it has often been done in the name of Christian love.

We cannot simply equate God's love with Christ's supreme act of sacrificial giving on the cross. This isolates the act from the inner motivation. Christ's death is not martyrdom for its own sake, which he simply must perform. The event of the cross is a healing act because it is freely chosen. Within the triune intimacy, Jesus knows the cost of obedience yet for the joy set before him, he gladly endures the cost (Heb. 12.2). He freely gives his life and bears our sin. To collapse agape into an ethic of giving replaces the reality of God's being-in-love with an abstract principle of sacrifice. The equipoise of Jesus's love for the Father and being loved by the Father is the reality out of which both the passionate giving and receiving of love emerge. It is the divine alternative to giving out of emptiness in order to be filled or out of the hunger to win approval.

Numerous Scriptures suggest that Jesus is equally at home

with the other side of love's rhythm. He openly receives passionate gifts from others without embarrassment, whether it is Mary's tearful anointing of his feet with oil, or the extravagant gifts and hospitalities of publicans and sinners. As a deer longs for living water (Ps. 42) so Jesus rises early to pray, or in freedom walks away from the clamouring crowds in order to restore his thirsty soul in intimacy with his Father. He commends Mary's need to be nurtured and sit at his feet, and gently rebukes Martha's serving because it has become compulsive and critical. Having become stuck in the giving gear, she is unable to shift into stillness and directly receive nurture herself.

Mr and Mrs Right

But you and I are unbalanced, sinful people. The harmony of love in Jesus is a stranger to us. As with desiring, our giving of love can go profoundly askew. Does this mean that in romantic love we are always prone to marry the wrong person? Should I try to learn from my mistakes, cut my losses and hope to make a better decision 'the next time around'?

Certainly, to acknowledge my imbalanced style of loving reminds me that I do not with intellectual deliberation walk into love. I fall. Conscious reasons are swept along by unconscious needs and social conditioning. Suppose a daughter grows up in a family in which her father is gentle and adaptively gives support and care, more so than, say mother, who is rather busily efficient in running the household. What if in time she finds herself falling in love with a man who is much more assertive and directive than her father, who aggressively seeks out what he wants in life and intends to find it. At first, this is a rather exciting and dramatic change, especially as she is the object of his passionate longing and firmness of purpose. It also allows the daughter to assume that gentle, adapting role her father has modelled to her over many years and which she now has the pleasure of enacting for another.

But as time wears on, the daughter who is now a wife may find herself missing the receiving of a more adaptive and flexible giving of affection. She increasingly feels undernourished and unvalued by her partner who now appears overly focused on his preferences whether at home or at work. She becomes resentful and adept at interpreting her partner's purposefulness as selfishness. The ideal partner has become the wrong partner. Was he always 'wrong' or does she need to acknowledge that her needs and skills in giving care are wearing thin in the absence of the gentle nurturing provided in her previous care network?

If in my family home, the balancing act of giving care is over-developed by one partner and being served and cared for by the other, I will usually identify with one and ignore my need for the other. Suppose I am drawn to and fall in love with someone very responsive to my side of the balance. The more I have identified with one part of love (to serve and to cherish or to receive and to be cherished) the more strongly I will be drawn to my opposite. Suppose I was not deeply attached to or identified with either parent, one being too smothering, one too distant? I may feel like an emotional orphan and naturally may respond strongly to someone who comes along as a very nurturing partner. But once obstacles are swept away with the arrival of marriage, we do not live happily ever after. One begins to react to 'over-nurturing' and seek distance. One may also react to elements of distancing, in the same person, and anxiously cling. The nurturer feels confused and rejected. Erotic bonding alone is inadequate to remedy this.

There are many possible imbalances we can find ourselves repeating. Perhaps both come from homes where we were 'left alone' because parents over-invested and over-attached to careers outside the home. Initially, we bonded joyfully to one another, but as friction arose, we replicated our parents' pattern and increasingly invested ourselves in careers, or one of us in the children, where our care-giving meets less resistance. We wake up one morning, realize we have become strangers, and despite the other, feel starkly alone.

One can see how romance as the magnetic attraction of polar opposites works well at first. But eventually, the dominant-submissive model may create resentments. Unless the community of love becomes more mutual, unless skills at giving and receiving are developed by both partners, that unacknowledged or undeveloped part of the daughter who needs caring will rise up and insist, perhaps very childishly, on being noticed on occasions and places other than at bedtime. Her partner may be shocked to hear that his 'dynamic leadership' is experienced frequently as boorish insensitivity. He may be hurt and irritated. Her protests at feeling trampled are experienced simply as nagging. His ideally adaptive partner is no longer so ideal or adaptive. Without fully realizing it, he may nostalgically long for someone who will once more be excited and attracted to his now devalued and repellant pole. After all, Prince Charming was schooled in the art of charm, not the art of kindness or fidelity.

Warring Factions: The Competitive Conflict

Probably the climactic pressure placed on romantic love is that for many of us it is here alone where society allows tenderness and gentleness to be experienced. Elsewhere tenderness is a sign of weakness or mental deficiency. Small wonder that even in this domain, romantic love's tenderness and courtesy is overwhelmed by the competitive ethos of power: dominance and submission, dependency and conquest. It is very tempting to use romantic love in service of an immature self's unsound demands to dominate or to be pampered. Our primordial romantic images of a damsel in distress and a knight in shining armour are taken one step further in a domestic setting, namely, someone needs to rule the castle and someone needs to be the servant. In a competitive world of bosses, authority, and status, it is consoling to have a place where our wills are done and we are served and obeyed. The servant may be a willing victim for there lies not far beneath the surface for many of us the secret wish to have someone take care of us and protect us so we will not have to make hard career choices or difficult decisions so long as we do as we are told.

The very language of love exhibits war-like competitive tendencies. Indeed, our passion for war and romantic love are more closely linked than we wish to admit. Historically, as De Rougemont has shown, romantic love poetry made frequent use of military metaphors. The lover besieged his lady, delivered amorous advances, pursued her, and sought to overcome her defences. Ironically, once the lady surrendered, the knight became her prisoner as well as her conqueror.[5] But what disorders romantic love with a fundamental competitiveness is the constant rumour that success in the art of love as in war, depends on having the right skills, qualities, and accoutrements which must be acquired or purchased. We win at romantic love as at war, by our craft and power. This pushes love into a downward spiral of comparisons, jealousy, and rivalry. My romantic happiness hinges on maintaining my superiority of attractiveness over my competitors lest I am abandoned for a more attractive prize or forever threatened by a stronger suitor. Such love is not forever, but instead places me on a permanent state of alert in order to ward off my rivals and maintain a competitive edge. The situation amounts to a perpetual state of lawlessness and insecurity, for 'all's fair in love and war'.

Redeeming our Passions

In 1 Corinthians, St Paul describes how our experience of God's love alters the imbalances and distortions of our idealistic loves, both need-centred giving, and need-centred desiring, when he compares and contrasts some of the changes when we experience life within the sustaining agape relation between Father and Son, and not raw desirability (eros), nor an exhausting servitude and dependency.

Because agape is faithful, even unto death on a cross, love is not envious or jealous, fearing it will lose out. Whereas eros envies and inflates itself with illusions and expectations (paper dolls) of how my partner ought to delight me, agape does not exalt itself, it is not 'puffed up' (v. 4). Romantic love, inflated with its own longing, can and will betray others, but agape never fails. Romantic love can only affirm what I desire, but agape never seeks its own way in isolation. It affirms all of life, not just my personal agenda, not just joy and bliss, but sorrow and brokenness. Agape 'bears all things, believes all things, hopes all things, endures all things' (v. 7). Because my partner's goals and struggles are as important as my own, agape desires to support as well and is not fixated on being supported. Of course I can also exalt myself by being above receptivity, and hence like Martha, subtly dominating by always serving, never like Mary, kneeling to receive. Without the other side of love's rhythm in self-emptying and receptivity, the giving of wonderful gifts, even tongues, prophecy, and faith, can be noisy and self-congratulatory (v. 1).

You could say God's way of loving brings love out of the ideal world and down to earth, when life is not romantic, when I am balancing the budget, when the priorities of home and work need to be renegotiated, when the baby needs feeding in the middle of the night (again), when the other has disappointed me (profoundly), when we are wrestling with an unsettling mid-life change. This love is not forever demanding drama and rapture. It is willing to wash dishes, fix breakfast, work with another's mood swings and apparent unreasonableness. Agape is willing to amend eros's focus on my paper doll. It chooses to relate to real persons, not ideal ones. It seeks to encourage my partner to be truly herself, not merely to fit my expectations. As love for the creaturely, human, and fallible, agape weans me from regarding my partner as a goddess (or a witch). Rather agape commits me to the fundamental equality of the sexes. I dare not divinize a fellow creature and make him or her my centring goal.

Agape's faithfulness also causes me to look at other women, or men, in a new way. Whereas eros uses others as holders of my 'paper doll' ideal, agape teaches me that persons are more than mirrors of myself. When tempted or fascinated by an attractive presence, agape reminds me that I am in the mysterious presence of a unique creation of God, with its own story and purposeful journey. I dare not isolate one element of that network and seek to use it to my private satisfaction. When I am tempted to possess or abstract-out qualities which I admire, agape grants me a vision of the sacred value and unity of the whole person within the life story God has granted them. Such temptation is never wholly absent of course, but gazing through agape's interpretive lenses, it is not obsessive.

Reconciling Warring Members

Let us return to that worried question, do we always fall in love with the wrong person? Yes, we fall in love with someone whose positive qualities attract us though the hidden side of the same aspects may indeed repel us. The less I know and understand my particular balance, the more hidden my undeveloped side of loving, the greater will be my attraction to one polarity in my partner. The more I do not know or avoid my own hidden side, whether it be leading or being led, giving or receiving, working or relaxing, the greater my eventual reactivity when my strength in loving is frustrated or unrewarded. When the accumulated capital from our previous systems of love trickles to a halt, I may fall out of love with quite a hard landing. As divorce statistics reveal, this is the blunt finale of love for many. But with the intervening help of another kind of love, this hard landing may be transfigured by grace into love's baptismal purging and resurrection. Centuries ago in Italy, the poet Dante described the journey of romantic love's descent into hell, its cleansing, and the recovery of his beloved Beatrice in heaven. In *The Divine Comedy*, Dante interprets and describes romantic love as it undergoes loss, purification, and recovery as a parable of God the divine lover's love and recovery of us.

There is nothing novel in asserting that romantic love lifts us to the heights of joy, but less understood is that it does so by leaping over the pain, deprivation and disappointments we have accumulated along the way. Romance covers an abyss of accumulated need, twisted defences, and avoidant ways of coping. Meanwhile these wounds throb under the surface and for lengthy periods of time lie buried beneath diversions, child-rearing, church, and community duties.

Eventually a crisis erupts. She is at home alone with the children, her parents offer no support, and domestic management and child-rearing are crushing her. She feels once again like an abandoned, frightened child. He, meanwhile, struggles at his career to develop a sense of competence and skill in a competitive, status-seeking world of achievers, and is plagued by self-doubt. For months, years, he comes home desperately weary, and needing nurture, having given his all to the company without any assurance of success. She waits for his return with similar needs, sleep-deprived from caring for young ones. But coming together is an experience in mutual abandonment. Unfulfilled, unresolved hurts burst to consciousness with volcanic force. The prognosis for romantic love to endure is most unlikely without the intervention of a love both higher and deeper than mutual attraction. In its rapid erection of a 'bridge over troubled water', romantic love denies or by-passes humankind's misery. But God's love and ours must descend into the valley of shame and humiliation, wade even the dark river of death as well as ascend the mountain tops of exultation.

When pain and disappointment mock our hopes, wounded lovers may experience the full severity of fight and flight reactions. One lover's safety is found in fleeing to the hills of distance and detachment from the beloved, desperately in need of time and space to mend alone, independently. The other partner's flight to safety is in an utterly opposite direction. The flight, like the fight which precipitated the search for safety, is straight into the arms of the beloved. But the beloved has fled.

'All night long on my bed I looked for the one my heart loves; I looked for him but did not find him' (Song of Songs 3.1). This is indeed hell. And it is no less a hell for the one seeking quiet to hear the beloved crying for him at the very moment he most hungers for retreat. Desperate, the avoidant lovers tentatively move to console and reconcile, but no sooner is one vulnerable and open than the hurt and anger of love's disappointed expectations smother him once more. In failure and aloneness, couples separate, hoping they have learned from the tragedy, hoping against the statistical evidence that a new partner will not bring similar disappointment, that they will never return to this scene of sorrow. I do not suggest that divorce is never preferable to a habitually bruising, humiliating, quarrel of a marriage. There is scriptural evidence that divorce may be the only humane alternative. But I suggest that restoration may occur in the most humanly unlikely situations, whenever a peculiar kind of intervention occurs.

It is a cross-shaped interpenetration, whereby the one partner participates in a sacrificial embrace, understanding and receiving the hurt of the other into his own soul. The ache for touch and closeness, the craving for distance and withdrawal, are felt as his own. Within agape's intervention, he finds the freedom to share the fears he could not dare admit about measuring up to the job's responsibilities and winning the approval of his colleagues and bosses. She shares the fears of being left behind and forgotten. Both listen in quiet, respecting the hurt of the other too much to offer glib remedies. Emotionally naked, neither is ashamed.

Here in the wilderness, far from the festivity of wedding celebrity and fashion, romantic love is baptized into the death of Calvary. For those aware of and willing to receive this crowning act of grace, they lose their lives to find them again in a crucifying embrace shared within a broken community of two. The tragedy of romantic passion becomes transfigured into a divine comedy. Together we experience an echo of the passion of God.

This is how agape intervenes in romantic love, not as a principle of sacrifice, a status or a reward for doing or believing the right things, but as sharing in the reality of God's inner life, a completed reciprocity of cruciform love, interrupting my one-sidedness, my wounded inflation or deflation. When the Son reached out in incarnate descent, death, and resurrection, he made a free exchange of sin and twisted pride for grace and humble love. The reality of his intervention touches my story as the Spirit uses pastors, friends, and counsellors to summon and support me as I participate in the Father and Son's passion to love and to heal. In a fresh Pentecost, the Spirit incorporates me personally into the history of the Son's mission of love.

Uninterrupted, romantic love prefers the 'paper doll' ideal. But this will break and collapse as reality inevitably crashes us to the shores of life's rocky edges and jagged inconveniences. It needs to be rescued or else our lives break up and flounder on a sea of ideals. The fact is that real people like you and me are messy. We offer resistance to love. But it is this messy earth, these imperfect friendships and marriages, that God loves and that he gives us to love.

It is God's good will that it should be difficult yet possible for lovers to love the real, not simply an image of perfection temporarily stuck onto someone. God's free self-giving from out of his inner life wins and frees me to transfer my loyalty from ideal people (my paper dolls) to embracing and being embraced by real people. Admittedly these loving embraces may take the shape of a cross. There is inevitably a dying to self which will be no stranger to pain. But beyond the pain and the cross, are rumours of resurrection. The Gospel declares that this dying is not an annihilation, but a transfiguring of the self, a severing and putting to death of the old self so that a new self may be reborn in union with the crucified and resurrected Christ. And the only way I discover if the rumours of glory are true is by taking up my little cross daily and following Him.

Notes

1 Quoted in Kelsey, Morton and Barbara, *Sacrament of Sexuality*, (Element, 1991), p. 131.
2 Dr Ken Magid, and Carole A. McKelvey, *High Risk, Children Without A Conscience*, (Bantam, 1989), p. 271.
3 Anders Nygren, *Agape and Eros*, (SPCK, 1982), p. 201.
4 C. S. Lewis, 'The Weight of Glory', *Transposition and other Addresses*, (Geoffrey Bles, 1949), p. 21.
5 Denis De Rougemont, *Passion and Society*, (Faber, 1962), p. 244.

3

Family Love:
Love's Balancing Act

Long before romantic fires are kindled, we have our first experiences of love in our families. As infants we experience mother's tender cuddles and warm, fresh milk. If we are fortunate, we soon encounter father's distinctive masculine affection as well as the companionship and camaraderie of brothers and sisters. But as C. S. Lewis has reminded us, if charity begins at home, so does uncharity. G. K. Chesterton once suggested that the true Victorian heresy was the hypocrisy of sentimentally idealizing domestic life as the highest value, as in 'A man's home is his castle', while the middle classes sent their children away to boarding-school and the poor had theirs sent to the workhouse or the factory. The young priest in Georges Bernanos' novel, who painfully unearths agonizing family conflicts, writes in his diary: 'How glibly we talk about "family life" . . . We ought to say many prayers for families. Families frighten me. May God be merciful with them.'[1] As a pastor I am awkwardly aware that it is much easier to preach about family love than to live a healthy domestic life.

Eventually, the soaring satisfactions of romantic love descend to the earth of routines, practicalities, and the managing of domestic detail. We discover that we are not alone with one another in our new marital home. In addition to romantic passion, partners bring to their new home the psychic patterns, and inner imbalances, from their initial experience of family love which must be blended within their newly acquired intimate relationship. Robert Bly bluntly reminds us that what we wanted in our family of origins, we still want. So the husband is hoping to receive the fathering and mothering he didn't receive; the wife seeks these also and brings this to the husband. We transport

36

and then unload these unmet, unacknowledged needs, and in anxious hope pile them in front of our partners. So large is the load, we easily lose sight of the other. Blame and disappointment mount.

To understand how family love works, gets stuck, and gets unstuck, it may help to think of several different energy systems which interact to create an 'emotional superhighway' on which flows the giving and receiving of love. Being aware of the traffic patterns we have brought to the marriage in terms of need and frustration can help us discover ways to renegotiate present road-blocks. The descriptions which follow are neither definitive nor exhaustive but suggestive of the complex road-works of energy systems along which family love journeys.

Negotiating Interior Systems

Impingement and Detachment: Too Much and Too Little

We already have seen that even as the desire of eros can be greedy, so the giving of philia or domestic love can be out of balance, controlling or aloof. It is more than a linguistic accident that 'mother' and 'smother' remind us of maternal love's tendency toward possessiveness and control. On the other hand, 'father' and 'farther' hint at the sadly familiar experience of emotional distance and lack of paternal affection in many homes.

Whether we quietly sit down to breakfast, or stand and pace with a bowl of cereal, whether we are getting ready for school or work or bed, there exists a desire for companionship and closeness and the desire for personal space, distinct identity, and individual development. Family love is the finely balanced harmony of being close and connected while also being distinct and separate. Too much closeness becomes a possessive, grasping, and domineering memory of desire now crippled by anxious need. This is not intimacy, but absorption. Donald Winnicott has used the word 'impingement' to describe this feature of family care-giving, namely, to meet another person's need in a manner and time which the recipient does not want and which causes him to shrink back within himself in retreat.[2] The opposite polarity from absorption is detachment. This is father with his face in the newspaper. Or it is mother compulsively substituting physical items (food, drink, work, sex) for emotional support and sensitive attunement. A family system may contain the inherent instability of a withdrawn, retreating person and a lonely, pursuing partner. When the separateness and aloofness of the retreating member becomes dominant, it leads to isolation and divorce.

Pursuing and Being Pursued

Emotionally, Mary was a neglected child who brought a fear of rejection and abandonment to all her relationships. Unfortunately her fear tended to create the situation she dreaded. In contrast, John, her husband, had been doted on by his family, the centre of attention. He had to move away to find his own way. But to whom did he find himself attracted? Mary, who marked him out of the crowd, and made him the centre of attention in her little world, and pursued him. At first John felt 'at home' again in a hostile world. Then all too soon he found himself once again seeking distance in his newly acquired intimate relationship of marriage. Meanwhile, Mary's nagging nightmare of abandonment was close to becoming reality.

It seems that in domestic love relations, the more the anxious lover pursues, the more the loved object seeks distance. An anxious parent urgently seeking to be closer to the adolescent child may succeed, temporarily. But the pursued child feels smothered and finds ways to increase the distance. A parent's fear of loneliness and abandonment sparks off a child's anxious need not to be a clone, but to establish her own personality. The mistake here is to assume that one person's love need is identical to another's. If one anxiously pursues closeness, it is wrongly assumed that must be what the other really needs as well. But to assume our needs are the same is a symptom of poor listening. The more the pursuer pursues, the more the distancer distances.

Sometimes distancing springs from my frustration at failing to solve my partner's problem. Instead of following St Paul's strategy of weeping with those who weep, I try to silence my partner's weeping, by removing the problem for them. My weeping partner does not feel blessed, but unaccepted in mourning, inferior to the non-weeping, problem-solving partner.

Not truly understood or supported, my partner is angry and feels patronized. I am hurt and with self-pity look elsewhere to bestow my patronage.

This conflict reminds us that we cannot reduce family love to cosy feelings of closeness. Love, unlike absorption, allows others to have their own feelings which may stand in contrast to our own. Love, unlike comfortableness, accepts conflict as a basic part of God's design in making each of us different and distinct. We all see the world through our unique framework. If I am free to be open and acknowledge that I feel a need to be closer, you are also free to declare your need for more space. Neither of us tries to make the other feel guilty for not having identical feelings to the other. As peers, not experts, we grant one another permission to explore honest and caring ways to find patterns of closeness and distance which equally respect one another's honest feelings. Conflict becomes not a competition which one of us must win and one must lose, but the ongoing retuning of intimacy, the discovery of our individuality within a communion of different, but equally valued members.

Should the problem-solving partner begin to acknowledge his anxious need to give care, he shall come face-to-face with his own limits and needs. As he ceases nervously fixing, but begins to weep with the one who is weeping, he enters into Jesus's passion for those who mourn. Ironically, this acknowledgement of weakness and limits enables his partner to feel valued and supported. Once the mourner feels truly cared for, not patronized, they both discover a new freedom to mobilize their own resources and find the courage to take up their own cross and find the narrow path. They can do this because they have been accompanied to the place of loss or limit and been granted permission without shaming or condemnation to grieve whatever has been lost, in the presence of love.

Closely related to the pursuer-pursued relation is the helper-recipient connection. Some of us are born givers and helpers. That is how we adapted to our families. We served. Perhaps we were the first-born and were groomed to be daddy's and mummy's little helper. We function in most relationships as helpers or care-givers. However, there is usually one hidden area or relationship where part of us cries out to be coddled and nurtured. Here we may feel deeply hurt that we have not been so nurtured. As a result, in this unexamined area, we are vulnerable to an addiction or a hidden and dishonest relationship.

Others of us may have grown up as 'helpees' or recipients, especially if one or two helpers were already in place and older. We were fumbling about, awkwardly trying to tie our shoes, so big sister tied them for us. We could not seem to get ready on time for the school bus, so mother in haste got out the car and drove us. We did not understand exactly how to write that essay, so big brother wrote it for us and mother typed it. What is hidden is the longing and need to assert ourselves and be independent. Unfortunately, this can emerge in inappropriate and frightening ways. Another imbalance occurs when 'helper' parents are over-committed outside the home, at church or other volunteering service, leaving children with left-overs. In all these situations, the unvarnished admission of imbalance in the presence of unsentimental and unconditional grace provides the missing quality of nurture and guidance which restores us from our detour back to the journey into mature development.

Returning to the Scene of the Crime

Every family is a living history with fault lines connecting us to our unresolved past. When I begin a new family, I bring to it the emotional world of my childhood family. John Bowlby's work on child development suggests that the single most important factor in personal maturity is the security of knowing one's parents are accessible and will be responsive to our needs.[3] If that availability feels uncertain or impinges rather than nurtures, our growth is plagued by anxiety and insecurity. But to the degree one parent smothers or another is aloof, confusions and loss of confidence in love arise. Love becomes something in doubt and under threat. I am ever striving to make the proper adjustments to others who have set down the rules and conditions by which care is won. This is most graphic in children whose parents use threats to control behaviour.

Threats to withhold love can be very stark indeed, including the threat of being sent away to boarding-school, the parent leaving home or even suicide. Naturally this heightens a child's anxiety and fear. Preoccupied with his unsatisfactory relationships, the child is too anxious to be able to relax in himself, concentrate on learning, and be interested in discovery. The more the parent threatens abandonment, is inaccessible, or unsupportive, the more the child anxiously clings to and desires the wrongly responsive parent. Ironically, the very person who frightens or frustrates us, we long for and cling to, for fear of abandonment. We also may identify with and internalize his or her worst pattern of behaviour.

In bringing such an inner emotional world to marriage, I unconsciously will find myself stuck in or attuned to reproducing the same fears and anxieties which I knew in childhood, for example, by my choice of partner (inaccessible or threatening) or by my provocative behaviour creating a climate where abandonment becomes a real possibility. Thus the sins of the childhood family are revisited upon the next generation. It is as if we find a way to return to the scene of the crime because until we resolve this primary wound, we cannot take further steps into mature love. We are like a computer which is jammed and cannot proceed until the correct instructions release us for further processing.

Keith came from a home where father was married to his career and absent from home. Father compensated for his emotional emptiness at home by a life-style of infidelity. Because this left his wife systematically starved for affection, she in turn anxiously pressured Keith for something of the support and affection she lacked from her husband. Her suicide during his later teenage years left Keith alienated from his father and isolated in his guilty wonderment of what he might have done to rescue her, if only he had been more sensitive. Several years into his own marriage and success in his career, he too would find himself deeply attached to work, increasingly distancing from his increasingly needy wife and, much to his horror, enmeshed in a series of infidelities himself. For Keith, the journey out of this destructive inherited pattern began in therapy as he was granted permission without blame or shame to acknowledge and mourn his loss of fatherly care-giving instead of repeating it with his own wife and children, through acting out his father's behaviour in his own life. His rejecting and distancing from his mother's needs and guilt over her death became translated into his marriage as an exaggerated awareness of and sense of responsibility

for his wife's needs. But the persistent linkage of his wife with
his mother's desperation only repelled him from closer contact
with her. He began to understand how the cumulative deprivation and emotional separation from home, in the form of
abandonment by his father and impingement by his mother,
had left him highly vulnerable to the seduction of physical
closeness without mature relationship.

Piece by piece, the puzzle of his chaos began to be put
together. In the presence of unsentimental grace, he was
finally able to explore the vacuums and patterns without being
made to feel ashamed and humiliated into hiding from both
his desperate behaviour and emotional neediness hidden
behind an outwardly successful public career. Mourning his
losses, he began to experience freedom to bond with his adult
family and not repeat the cycle. By consciously returning to
the scene of the crime with a counsellor who neither shamed
nor coddled him, he was free at last to explore and grieve his
loss. As a result, he no longer compulsively repeated the crime
upon himself and his family.

Idealizing and Demonizing

The move from our childhood to our adult family tempts us to
idealize our parents in one of two ways. The first way is to
positively idealize our parents by putting them on a pedestal
and refusing to acknowledge their clay feet. Why do this?
Consider the posture of a young child gazing up at mother and
father. The parent is visually and physically a god-like figure,
with no limitations to wisdom, whose strength dwarfs the child's.
When they look down, smile, and value the child, we have our
first glimpse of what it feels like to hear the heavenly blessing,
'Well done, thou good and faithful servant'. When we disobey or
fail to delight, in those disapproving looks, rebuking voice, and
corporal punishment, we have our first foreboding glimpse of
the yawning mouth of hell.

In such a frame of mind, the child assumes the parent is
correct and he is at fault. He feels guilt and shame when their
ideal for him and his reality is far apart. It is his fault. He feels
ashamed of the ugly gap which he seems to embody. But suppose father's expectations are unreal or his own negligence has

led to the gap between his standards and the child's shoddy performance of duty? What if mother was too critical, too impatient? Every parent fails at some vital point. To the extent we accept their standards, we live as a guest, or as a prisoner, in their emotional world of expectations and ideals. And living in their inner world causes us to be angry and resent the cause of the gap between these ideals.

One way of dealing with this gap is the process of idealizing and identifying with our parents' vision of life and defending them against any suggestion that they maintained their virtue at our expense. They were not lazy or limited. We were. Each time mother is sad or angry, it is our fault. Mum is good. We are bad. We learn to interpret that part of us which is angry or hurt as naughty, never mother or father for impatience and limits in love. They only are angry and punish us for our own good. Once we become parents, we too shall identify our anger with our parents' as righteous wrath, our neglect as benign as theirs. Our children must learn to conform to our parental will.

The other way to idealize parental authority as a child is to despise it. In this way we are enthralled to our parents not as idols, but as demons. Every remembrance of parental anger or discipline is interpreted as cruel and malicious. In retrospect, I view my childhood angers not only as understandable, but as always justified, all childhood desires as appropriate.

This way of idealizing our parents has learned unconsciously that the best defence is a good offence. We find that blaming or aggressive reactions are less painful, more efficient ways to counter parental discipline and sweep our slate clean of any self-condemning thoughts. It propagates the cult of the perpetual victim: 'It's your fault.' In coming to terms with the pain of our past history, we are armed with the aid of a new theory. We can now win the competition with parents by transferring the powerful mantle of authority exclusively to the child. Now instead of the child being the one who is always wrong, it is the parent. Whenever my parents, upset or alarmed at my behaviour, attempted in an anxious way to force an adjustment on my part, the child part of me refuses to be reconciled to this 'cruel' act and person. The child part of me has become as totalitarian and exacting as the parental model was once. This demonizing propensity intensifies beyond calculation whenever there has approached a significant level of abuse, emotional or sexual, in the childhood home. The pressure that has built up either to identify with or despise is so great that special support and intervention is required if we are to break out of this twin-celled prison.

The more the child simply emotionally identifies the parent as saint or demon, the more likely as a parent himself he will interpret his own discipline either as from the very hand of God or as being utterly selfish. When a parent, once dominated as a child, decides never to do such to his children, he identifies exclusively with the childlike part of the family system. Soon he may find himself being dominated once again in his new family, this time by his own children's undisciplined expressions and unlimited, uninterpreted demands. If a parent identifies solely with his parents and the parental role, he will simply apply the domineering style of his parents to his own children. On the other hand, if he identifies exclusively with the child's feelings, he assumes that parental pedagogy is always to blame, and the developing child need take no responsibility. He perpetually denies his own limitations in loving, pointing the blame at his parents or now at his new family group. More hopeful, is a respectful dialogue between different members of a family, not a totalitarian theory granting parents or children absolute authority. Also more hopeful is a parent who is discovering a kind of authority which is eager to share power rather than hoard it to himself.

Domination and Chaos

In tears, a pre-adolescent child refuses to eat dinner, saying it is 'yuck'. An adolescent child with military intensity marches down the hall, shouts and slams the door announcing he is going out to visit friends, not to tend the garden, as requested by mother. Such strong reactions arise from a long process, a history in which countless disagreements have built up and not been resolved peacefully. Should parents simply flow with the chaos or fasten a firm lid on it? How can a parent negotiate liveable space between chaos and domination in managing conflict?

To simply suggest that children express themselves leads to an anarchy of shouting, or physical force on the part of some member of the conflict, normally the parent until adolescence when nature grants children the increasing opportunity to take this role. On the other hand, the old adage, 'If you can't say anything nice, don't say anything', while tempting, ignites a slow fuse of frustration in which rage eventually explodes or creates an unbridgeable chasm. Whether it has to do with eating vegetables, doing chores, or arranging schedules, neither parents nor children need be bullied or blamed. The goal is to prepare children for a responsible adulthood which arranges work and play, and time alone and time together in such a way that these are fairly shared, and not the exclusive role of parents or children. The means towards this end cannot be verbal or physical coercion, for these means contradict our goals. Shouting begins and interruptions are incessant because when we want something, this has not been directly stated or recognized, so our frustration is channelled into aggression or the indirect acting out of mis-behaviour. When these behaviours happen, as they inevitably shall, we have a God-given opportunity to confess our own sins, not another's, resist the tendency to blame others, and restate our goal.

In the opening conflict between a playful dad who left the house a mess and a tired mother returning from choir practice, the 'attack and blame' strategy of one parent could have easily evoked a defensive, 'You misunderstand me, I was only playing with the kids' response. This firmly sets both in the rightness of their ways. Children observing this competitive blame game learn to find ways to make the blaming label stick and to defend themselves well against their critics. Ought dad be blamed for neglecting the clean up? Ought the children be blamed, and made to feel guilty, for playing with dad instead of terminating play earlier and beginning to tidy up?

Once the blaming strategy is operating and someone who is verbally weaker at self-defence gets stamped with the blame, conflict is snuffed out at the price of sacrificing one person's honour or place: they are designated the naughty one, the lazy, the selfish. But the process of being a family is profoundly misunderstood when someone is labelled as the cause. The solution lies in confessing our sins, not others', re-negotiating play and work responsibilities, finding co-operative new ways, that renounce the competitive framework of fighting for limited resources. Parents and children both have legitimate longings to develop gifts and talents. Parents and children both have a desire to give and sacrifice lest they become unbalanced givers: secretly resentful, secretly earning heroic status; or unbalanced receivers: weak, needing constantly for other people to adapt to their agenda, incompetent, always needing to be rescued or entertained.

We are all predisposed to play one of these roles: omnicompetent fixer and rescuer; or ever-needy, 'entertain me, feed and water me, make me happy'. Each role comes along with a fully imprinted programme to blame or to use other people in our family, and in the larger family of nation and world. Learning a proper balance means learning to recognize the role we are playing, distinguishing one role from another, and letting go or sacrificing our identity and sense of worth from that outer role and behaviour. The sharing of roles, the acquiring of a balance between giving and receiving, activity and quiet, work and play, is the great project of family life. When power and responsibility are more shared, fewer explosions arise. Rebellion becomes unnecessary. When play and work are equally valued and seen as life-enriching, there is less jealousy between, and more respect for, a new balancing of responsibilities and a new respect for different stages of development.

Redeeming the Polarities: Love's New Creation

Honouring

The new world created by love's intervention recreates our inner systems from a competitive to a nurturing environment. Hence the mandate of Christian nurture is not to idealize, nor to demonize but to honour our parents. As long as I reside emotionally in an ideal world of ideal parents, to 'honour' means never making any critical appraisal of the way it really feels to live within the ideals of my parents and never to develop my own world view. I have deactivated any sense that my parent is part of a painful, sinful system. Why? Because it is too scandalous an idea, threatening my very survival if I acknowledge the limitations of my parents' capacity to love. To avoid this heresy, I idealize them and my childhood: 'They did it for my own good. They meant well.' This hides rather than honours my real parents behind an idealized memory for it refuses the maturing process of owning my wounds, facing the process of forgiving my parents and becoming reconciled to them. This hiding may lead to a habitual need to please or defer to my partner, employer, ethnic group or community. I overwork, over-adjust, for any conflict activates the old assumption: 'It's my job to accommodate to your standards and expectations.' Alternatively, I may always play a parental role in relationships, never working alongside as a peer, only as boss, lest I put myself in the hated role of submission to another.

Honouring in biblical faith has a surprising quality, as when God honours us by calling his people to repentance. For children, the surprise in honouring is when I recognize that, rather than idealizing my parents as faultless, I can give a better, more honest gift of forgiving them when through their own fear and anxiety, they misused their authority and were neglectful or coercive. On the other hand, as a parent, I am warned not to 'provoke my children to wrath' (Eph. 6.4), by blaming my children in a causal way for my moods of anger or anxiety. I will see these emotions not necessarily as righteous, or as evil, but will learn to acknowledge my angers and disappointments as instinctive responses to children's behaviour that was not what I had wanted. And I will learn to grieve my impatience as a symptom of my own impoverished capacity for love. I will confess my limits, not defend, deny, or blame them on my children.

But in learning to honour my children, I will come to suspect that much of my anger has less to do with respecting my children than with an anxious grasping after a technique with which to control their behaviour. Sadly, this often used tool of control becomes the chief creator of rebellion or prison-cell compliance and misdirects the child's energy in becoming angry at me in reaction to my anger at them. Energy is misused seeking revenge rather than creatively solving the problem which aroused my parental anger in the first place. Perhaps the wisest honour I can bestow as a parent is to embark on a transition in my identity as controller or manager to one who grants ever-increasing areas of freedom and creativity so that my children will learn to develop their talents and creatively learn the difficult art of responsible choices in the expanding areas of life which they encounter as life progresses.

Consider the difference in emotional tone between issuing an order or command: 'Tidy that room or you cannot play today!' and the granting of permission: 'As soon as your room is tidy you are free to play.' Or instead of angrily saying (again): 'Don't interrupt!', I say firmly but with empathy and a bit of sadness: 'Son, you have a choice. If you continue to interrupt, then I'm afraid you are going to spend some time out in your room.' The latter approach shares responsibility, 'You have a choice', and expresses both a preference to enjoy their company, and a willingness, not to inflict harm or to punish, but to enforce the appropriate consequences of incivility, namely temporary non-participation in our small community. Setting honest boundaries and teaching basic standards of courtesy and ethics need not be harsh nor punitive. Indeed such methods only instruct others that power calls the tune. The day shall come when power hoarded, not shared and given over to those in our care, shall be unceremoniously snatched by those who have been tutored in our manner and method more than we realized.

Forgiving

Adults who as children were emotionally or physically abused by their parents may find the prescription of forgiveness a bitter pill to swallow. It may feel like the final act of divine bullying ('You must forgive!'), not the sole antidote to eliminate poison from our system. Some prefer no relationship to a relationship in which I 'must', 'should', 'ought to' forgive. How can one move from the legalism of 'having to' forgive to the grace of freely forgiving, which alone restores us to health and makes recon-ciliation possible, 'that our days may be long on this earth'? Why forgive another unless they first are sufficiently repentant and contrite? It is so tempting to return an eye for an eye and a tooth for a tooth all the conditional love or neglect which I have suffered, until my debtor pays me the last farthing I am owed (Matt. 5.26).

   The process of letting go, giving over, or forgiving, our griev-ance and hatred will be an echo in our experience of Jesus's own passion and the grounds for the mercy he expresses on the cross: 'Father, forgive them, for they know not what they do'(Luke 23.24). How does forgiveness disarm my hatred and make me lay down my guns of revenge and punishment? The process of for-giveness has been powerfully expounded by Smedes and others (we hurt, we hate, we heal).[4] But surrounding this process, we are aware of a numinous quality. This is hinted at in the motion picture *Field of Dreams* where an embittered son hears a mysterious voice telling him to build a playing-field where the crops are grown, even though financially he needs the acreage to pay the mortgage. Having taken this awkward risk, levelled the crops and built the playing-field, eventually a youthful stranger ventures into the field. Slowly it dawns on the son that this is his father as he was before life had punished and degraded and worn away his own dreams. He sees a shy, gentle young man, eager to play. The son experiences a side of his father which he rarely knew and had long since forgotten. He begins to sympathize with the hard things, the disappointments, the long hours, which made him into an ill-tempered, absentee dad. The son's anger and rebellion are transmuted into pity and understanding of his father's pain and lack of nurture. He now sees the faint and fleeting acts of paternal love not merely as feeble and inadequate, but as caring movements against a tragic backdrop of apathy. Their meagreness is now not merely infuriating but also deeply tragic and sad. Their rarity and potential left unenjoyed are occasions of grief for a father and son's mutual loss. A new tenderness and caring now emerges to inform his own parenting. Facing the history of his loss and undergoing the process of forgiving, is the opposite of either form of romanticizing or demonizing. As a result, the son learns from within that God demands of him, not another sacrifice, but only mercy (Matt. 12.7). For mercy alone echoes the humbling honour God bestows on all fathers and sons, and mothers and daughters, when they confront and confess their failures and limitations in loving.

The Family as Idol?

Within the New Testament there are glimpses of a profound change in the identification of family love with exclusivity and narrowness. The family as life-focus is a golden calf which the Bible topples. Again and again Jesus wrestles to extend love beyond a limited circle of the nuclear family, and tribal and ethnic loyalty. It is of a piece with the Old Testament prophets' challenge to Israel when she habitually interprets her chosenness not as a light to the gentiles but as self-congratulation. We see

Jesus breaking out of these limits when he qualifies his parents' traditional authority by lingering in the temple in order to be about his Father's business. The cryptic dialogue with his mother at the wedding feast in Cana further exposes an expansion of boundaries as he tells his mother: 'Woman, what have you to do with me? My hour has not yet come' (John 2.4). When the next moment Mary gives word to the servants to do whatever Jesus requests, she too is in the process of experiencing a transition in roles and authority. Shortly thereafter he stretches traditional family loyalty and identity to its breaking point when he declares to both family and community that his mother and father and sister and brother are those who do his will. When his outspoken comment regarding gentile dogs is juxtaposed with a woman's humble response and believing heart, perhaps we are witnesses to an experience within Jesus himself of the untwisting of the ancient ethnic bigotry which runs in human veins. An act of healing follows (Matt. 7.6). Wider yet are the boundaries of love extended from ethnic loyalties to our rivals and competitors in the story he tells of the good Samaritan (or, depending on one's local expression and projection of the enemy, the good Communist in the United States, or the good Capitalist in Castro's Cuba).

For those with eyes to see, such incidents reveal that deep within Jesus there is being burned into his humanity the knowledge that every family on earth is named in heaven, and has been made according to the purpose and intention of his Father. He journeys into this mission more deeply each day as he proceeds towards Golgotha.

Untwisting not Disappearing

The young priest in Bernanos' novel has not overstated the problem. Families do indeed need our prayers. But how shall we pray for our families? That we be permitted to take revenge on those who trespass against us? That all be smooth sailing? That the sins of our fathers and mothers magically vanish from our inherited systems? This final prayer reflects a notion of salvation as an escape from the creaturely and earthly structure of dis-ease. It prays as if God never wore our broken, sinful humanity, but instead wore only a human tuxedo, and did not himself wrestle with these distorted patterns in his own family life with Joseph and Mary, with the twelve, and the Roman-occupied Palestine of his day.

Events such as Christ's lingering at the temple, his dialogue with Mary at the wedding, his re-defining the true nature of brothers and sisters and parents, reveal the baptism of family life into the depths of holy triune love. We see but glimpses and not formal programmes and prescriptions because these would seduce us into following outer roles without experiencing from within a transformation of the heart. But in these events we perceive enough to hear the call to be baptized into his baptism, which includes our notions and experience of family love in our homes, villages and nation-states. To have our ideas and ourselves baptized into his baptism means untwisting the ingrown and exploitative cultural patterns in the presence of holy love.

Untwisting is a cruciform pattern, not a disappearing act. This means we will learn, by grace, to pray in confession, 'Come Holy Spirit', that the living word of God would speak to us in judgement and grace, piercing us asunder to the joint and marrow, separating our legitimate needs from our greeds and compulsions, which are bottomless and which may drink homes and churches and entire continents dry. Praying this prayer brings us a growing confidence that as we play and work, the word of God will not feed unhealthy desires nor bless our repressive avoidance of the truth about our secret hearts. Instead the Spirit will grant us the cleansing pain of disclosing our distorted patterns. So profoundly does the Spirit honour us that he plants us into a family of the Holy Spirit, the Church, where the broken clay of our own family structures are in love acknowledged and compassionately reshaped through holy love.

So Peter, the assertive leader, has his feet washed by Jesus who leads by serving. Martha, the hard-working, organizing servant, is summoned to feed her soul by sitting quietly at Jesus's feet. The young, prodigal brother who searches unendingly for pleasure, and the elder brother who knows only duty, have both lived near the Father without knowing his heart. They too must discover the Father who in sovereign love accompanies me as I return home to his heart and discover my true identity and purpose hidden underneath my compulsive and dutiful serving or perhaps my unending pursuit of pleasure.

However, within our seamless web of diversions, duties,

routines, committees and causes, the endless noise of radios, stereos, televisions, videos, hi-tech games, telephones, and answering-machines, how do we hear anything remotely like a still small voice which would rightly orientate us on our journey home to God's heart? Only when we consciously elect to pursue silence and space where God's word meets us in the quiet of mutual listening which is prayer, in the open sharing of a caring group of soul friends, who listen in respectful silence, and not with advice and interpretation, or in confession to a caring pastor, priest or guide. In these places and nowhere else can we freely and without condemnation disclose the tensions we have been avoiding, discover the angers and fears we have consciously tried to ignore but unconsciously acted out in our relationships. In prayer, in silence, and in holy communion we may relax and let go of the blame game, relinquish our fascination with our outer critics, and allow our distorted inner patterns to be disclosed before the gracious atmosphere of God's unconditional love and forgiveness which frees us. We are learning to expose ourselves in vulnerability and openness to a judgement which is for the sake of healing.

Mercifully, we not only survive but grow through the true self-knowledge we acquire in the presence of Jesus Christ. For in Jesus Christ there is not the mixed signal of 'yes and no' or 'maybe', 'but in Him it has always been "yes" ' (2 Cor. 1.19). As parents we are surprised to receive through our children a new start, exploring our imbalanced style of loving at the very time we are physically closer to the declining journey towards death. Grandparents, so I am told, receive even a further springtime of renewal and reconciliation when they have eyes to see and hands to receive this deeper gift of advancing years. This is the steadfast love which creates hope and courage for our adventures on the less travelled path of redeemed family love.

Perhaps the final surprise in redeeming family love is the earthly arena where families most thoroughly engage in this encounter, that is, the gathering of sinners which is the Christian Church. But before we examine this larger family, let us take a closer look at the 'smallest sociological unit of the Church'[5] (Bonhoeffer), that area on our map where romantic and family love interact.

Notes

1 Georges Bernanos, *The Diary of a Country Priest*, (Doubleday, [1937], 1959), p. 147.
2 Donald W. Winnicott, *The Child, the Family and the Outside World*, (Penguin, 1965), p. 223.
3 John Bowlby, *Attachment and Loss, volume 2, Separation: Anxiety and Anger*, (Penguin, [1973], 1985), p. 366.
4 Lewis Smedes, *Forgive and Forget: Healing the Hurts We Don't Deserve*, (Harper and Row, 1984).
5 Dietrich Bonhoeffer, *Sanctorum Communio*, (Collins, 1963), p. 155.

4

A Good Enough Marriage

The road from romantic attraction towards the freedom of a larger love has a lowly, narrow entrance beneath which one must stoop to enter: we call it marriage. With its inaugural vows we make promises of lifelong commitment, not whispered safely and cosily in a fantasy of secrecy, but real promises for all to hear, to live together as husband and wife until death slices us apart. Lest our passions cause us to become disorientated as we approach the signpost marked marriage, it is worth examining on our map the road systems which have led us towards marriage.

Marriage confronts us at the intersection of two great energy systems of love: family and parental love, and romantic love. At any crossroads, where roads intersect to make a new road, there is a leaving behind of a familiar path even as there is an entry into a new way. That leaving naturally involves a letting go, a death, in order to follow the new. Letting go implies both a grieving as well as a rejoicing at a new beginning. It is the old paradox of losing life in order to find a new life.

The initial path which leads towards marriage is family love. Its role in preparing us for marriage is immense. No one loves and gives and nurtures us like the family, like our parents give and love. Nor is any other love ever so one-sided in terms of who is in control. Parents initiate. They are older. They have the knowledge and the experience, not to mention the money. But the day comes when a man shall leave his mother as his primary care-giver and a woman leave her home and the two shall cleave to each other and become one. For parent-family love to retain its previous centrality only causes sadness and confusion. There is a mutual letting go here so a new life may emerge.

The other path which leads to marriage is romantic love. Though rather an upstart spring next to family love, the natural magic of mutual attraction and affection, crackling like electricity, longing for one another's presence, moves us passionately on towards the marriage altar. Let us not forget that God delights in romantic love. After all, he invented it. And in the days of Jesus's earthly ministry, he made wine, good wine for the wedding feast. Yet marriage is more than simply changing lanes and transferring from the family energy-system lane to the romantic lane on our 'emotional superhighway'. There is a death here too. Not to see this is to misunderstand Christian marriage profoundly. Here is a clue why many of our marriages are unwell and fragile.

For husband and wife romantic love is a sweet sacrifice they bring to the marriage altar as they do family love. Though romantic love is an exalted and glorious mood of life, we cannot control our moods or programme passion's permanence, try as we might. Romantic love whispers ultimate dedication but is universally notorious for failing to keep its promises. For every action, there is a reaction. He who falls in love, falls out. She is no different. One of the sadder phenomena of our age is the sheer havoc which many in our communities inflict upon themselves by relentlessly pursuing such mood-love, gaining it fleetingly, but then acquiring disappointment, betrayal and instability.

That is why Christian marriage places the passion of romantic love alongside and removes it from its centrality in order to bear witness that somehow this romantic love, which tastes so good and is so precious, must not stand exalted within the isolation of its own splendour. It cries out to stand alongside another passion, and another beauty which is more than romantically exhilarating. This is a splendour which has been crowned with thorns and crucified. The weakness in our love cries out for a deeper, more profound love to heal its limitations, to endure our mood swings, which holds fast when all is not very attractive or exciting. This love descends into hell it is so enduring. The point is that the romantic altar has been removed from the centre. But for that very reason the fire falls from heaven upon it unannounced and quickens it to life as the wind of the Spirit dances upon us. This is romantic love's pilgrimage into marriage.

Nothing else creates such a home for love to dwell within. For this love does not abandon us even in the valley of humiliation, failure and death. Nothing else creates such a context for love to mature than knowing the other person is unconditionally committed to us, in bad times, in sickness, emotional or physical, as well as in health and in abundance. This is crucial because love matures in the valley as nowhere else. But this happens only as we honour and do not despise the valley in absolute preference for ideal situations.

Here we cross the threshold into the healing heart of it all, the realism of Christian marriage. For it is grounded in the realism of God's love. Marriage is a pilgrimage into a love in which we may as well relax in the knowledge that every marriage is imperfect and ours will be no exception. None of us marries exactly the right person. We are all flawed and if we accept this, we can experience a marriage which nurtures us in solidarity with the atoning love that embraces and forgives sinners, not ideal people.

As long as we cling to our fantasy of the ideal man or ideal woman, so aflame are we with our passion we never come to know and love the real person. But as the apostle Paul told us long ago, it is better to marry than to burn. And the One in whose presence we are united in Christian marriage is he whose love for sinners enables us to experience love and forgiveness in real relationships, not be consumed by a longing for ideal ones. And such a three-fold cord is not easily broken. Daily we learn to love this sinner we made these great promises to on our wedding day. The real work and ongoing joy of marriage, like real prayer and real charity, shall be done, not by grand acts in front of crowds, but in secret, small, modest actions, rather complex and difficult at times.

The gift of agape means that rather than letting it alarm us, marriage offers us the unique gift of relaxing in the knowledge that our partner will not be perfect. Not now, not ever (on this earth, anyway). Agape gives us permission to relax in the grace that our partner will never perfectly satisfy all our hopes and dreams. Thank God. They were never intended for that. Rather, we may rejoice that by the mystery of grace we shall have not a perfect partner, but a good enough marriage for two sinners to enjoy . . . sharing hopes, disappointments, anger (perhaps taking this in turns), tears, and laughter. Christian marriage celebrates a love which has space in it to love the imperfect and give it room to grow. Through marriage we may share concretely in the love of Christ who has stretched beyond the perfection of heaven to touch us in the middle of all our contradictions, the arrogance of our strengths, and the fear of our weaknesses. Each day in moments romantic and moments quite unromantic, we put flesh and blood into our promises by giving to each other ongoing acts of caring, resurrected daily by forgiveness.

In this way Christian marriage participates in a new quality of life born from the dying seeds of romantic and family love. In so doing, Christian marriage bears witness to a trust and friendship grounded in Christian love's utter realism and faithfulness revealed in Jesus Christ. Thus does marriage testify to our families and our romances of an amazing grace which embraces, sustains, and forgives sinners.

A Helping Companionship

In rereading the creation story, it is worth noting that God does not pronounce his benediction 'this is good' on Adam until Eve is brought forth from his rib. Let us recall that God is not some monad of energy or will-power. If God in his innermost being as trinity is a differentiated relationship of love, is it surprising that to reflect or to be in God's image, Adam and Eve shall live within the differentiation and distinction carved into our humanity, male and female? It is within this relation that God considers his work complete and gives his blessing.

Certainly our humanity reflects God's image in many relationships of caring and creativity. A life of celibacy offers almost too many opportunities for intimacy and depth in relationships. Celibacy poses similar problems as married love with regard to maturity, with temptations to avoid or engage in self-destructive ways which imperil maturing love. Indeed the unlimited possibilities for intimacy are a major hurdle for the deepening of loving relationships. Some celibates dissipate their energies in too many superficial relationships; others in their lack of marital obligation to intimacy, retire within to a habit of unexpressed and unlived stagnation. Marriage with its unique balancing of physical and spiritual proximity, offers an unequalled opportunity to experience love in a faithful, lifetime partnership.

A Mutual Helping

However, not all kinds of help are helpful. When the Lord said, 'It is not good for the man to be alone. I will make a helper suitable for him' (Gen. 2.18), the key adjective is 'suitable'. What help can marriage partners give that is suitable and cause marriage to mature and what kind of help keeps the marriage in an infantile or arrested state of development?

Our first clue is St Augustine's comment on the creation of Adam and Eve, that woman comes not out of man's head to rule over him (that would be unsuitable or unhelpful help), nor out of his foot to be subservient (unhelpful help again), but out of his rib to be alongside as covenant partner, male and female. This is the suitable help God pronounces 'good'. As I was con-templating marriage, a friendly adviser of mine had not listened to Augustine when he said to me: 'A man needs to love and a woman needs to be loved.' Though this is partly true, it is laced with implicitly distorted pictures. What if one partner says, 'Dear, I'll be the brawn, you be the brains'? Or 'I'll be the head, you be the heart . . . I'll be the lover, you the lovee . . . me active, you passive . . . me brave, you admiring . . .' and on and on. These portrayals imply a primitive, one-dimensional dependence and identification with one pole of the dynamic of love. Such set roles have been maladaptive for some time and squander the opportunity marriage gives to become not symbiotic partners but whole persons in a companionship of love. Men need to be loved as well as to love. So do women.

Certainly in the infancy stage of our being-in-marriage, we often experience one of us as more confident at giving, one more gracious in receiving. We enjoy and feel glad to receive or to give care so gracefully and tenderly. But the goal of suitable help is not to be half a person, a specialist, but for each to develop mutual capacities to think and to feel, to give and to receive love.

Many of us have inherited a model of partnership that implies that one partner is to be skilled and competent in the place of work and the other in the home. In spite of its manifold failures and the nearly universal need for both partners to be employed in work, often outside the home, for too long the accepted role has remained for the man to focus and value his career to the point of over-investing in it. Often, when he returns home, he has almost nothing left to give, having squandered it in pursuit of that 'bitch-goddess', success. This can leave one's personal world precious near to shambles. The reverse is the common case for the woman. As a professional, a labourer, or a manager, husband and father would listen all day to clients and colleagues, but have no energy left to creatively listen and explore with his wife and his children. In some marriages, both partners may be overly attached to work and career and under-attached to home life. But for increasing numbers of us, the model of specialized identity and attachment, the male to the job, the female to the home, is no longer helpful. The challenge of this present generation is to redraw the map of work skills and home skills which respects the Genesis passage and Augustine's interpretive insight into how mutuality creates whole people. A closed and implicitly hierarchical role demarcation makes each of us dependent in one sphere, independent in another, not mutually intimate in either.

I am not suggesting that one member will not be better at cooking and another more able at balancing the budget. Often one will have skills which frankly are more financially marketable. But I am saying that it is important to learn how to feel as well as to think; important to learn skills and competence not just in earning a living, but in living a life: wisdom in being a father or a mother, competence in recovering one's own unresolved childhood conflicts through encountering them, and working them through in partnership with one's spouse and children. These skills are as crucial as the career outside the home for both husband and wife. Help that is mutual, not dependent, creates a new, more complex, organism–one flesh–in which both learn in marriage how to play as well as how to work.

Another clue about help that is suitable, which we learn to give and receive, comes from the New Testament, from St Paul's advice to the Christian community: 'Weep with those who weep. Rejoice with those who rejoice' (Rom. 12.15). Helping means weeping together and rejoicing together. For too long I fancied that helping my wife meant solving her problem for her, in effect, turning her from weeping to rejoicing. Some of us listen quite well for five minutes, or ten minutes and then, being helpers who sometimes need rather desperately to help, we proceed to give lovely little pearl-packed sermons of good advice: 'Buck up', 'Not to worry', 'It's worse in Sudan'. Or we burst inside with the need to do something for our partner which will solve their problem. But when our help is not received with sufficient gratitude, we pout or withdraw in hurt. We may take our helping energies to places where it feels more appreciated. The unwelcome fact is that such help arises out of my need to be a kind of spiritual Sean Connery, some ideal lover who smoothly finds the right word, the right touch, to move my partner over to the rejoicing side: 'She's not happy? Quick! Super-husband to the rescue, with the good word, the good plan.' But when helping arises out of my need to rescue, it is not good listening and it is patronizing. It is me being grandiose; it is her being rescued. 'Me-Tarzan, You-Jane.' It is full of subtle superiority and inferiority, not mutually creative problem-solving. No doubt this split role is deeply engrained from previous generations. One leaps to play the parental problem-solver role; one waits as a needy child to be rescued or perhaps resents such treatment. Unknown to our personal software is a disc on which problem-solving is a more mutual and shared endeavour.

The help that respects my partner and accepts my limits is weeping with, and exploring with my partner, as a peer and an equal, not a daddy (or a mummy). By being alongside, I support, explore, and encourage not as a superior being, for I am not, but through letting my partner know I will share, endure, and be alongside them in their perplexity and pain. This kind of respect and support enables a partner to mobilize their own resources, bear their own burdens, and do so trusting and having confidence that I believe in them and will stay alongside as they creatively resolve their conflicts, not having big daddy or omnicompetent mama do it instead. That is help in which our partner can find encouragement. That is helping, not dominating. This help begins to express a mutual companionship, not a dominating problem-solver and a submissive recipient.

For some of us it takes years to learn to offer and receive helpful help. Our partners may suffer long while we retool our helping machines from feverish over-activity or tepid under-functioning. But marriage is the sturdy vessel which weathers the storm of two people learning how to give suitable help, not subtly incapacitating or scolding. Marriage is the process of learning to make problem-solving not a burden but more like creative play, enabling each other to increase skills of intimacy at home and competence at work, without these two being hopelessly incompatible.

This brings us again to the realism of Christian marriage. How do we help one another in our many mistakes and failures? It is nothing to be ashamed of that a life together is more complex than our previous life apart. We undoubtedly will make mistakes as we foster and nurture this new self–two become one. Mistakes will be made as we learn the proper amount of distance and closeness which intimacy requires. Both parties get this wrong. It really does not matter who is the first one to lose a temper or the first to withdraw and close off because one feels misunderstood. One of us may cling too much. One may be too distant. It is no help apportioning blame, but it is help to learn to explore together without blame how it happened, to understand and adapt our responses in mutually respectful ways. For example, 'Do I really sound just like your mother when I ask you what you've been doing with yourself?', 'How does that make you feel?', 'I wonder where that slight condescending tone in my voice comes from?' Perhaps it is just a touch of shaming in your tone of voice but then our own inner amplification system acquired over a lifetime makes it sound much louder than it was. Who can know? There is no point in apportioning blame.

It is worth exploring why one naturally expresses annoyance or disappointment whereas the other naturally represses anger and holds the hurt within. When both are explored and not condemned, a deeper intimacy and respect can grow. The expressor's fear of being controlled or dominated based on previous experiences is acknowledged. The repressor's fear of rejection if someone reveals dissatisfaction is made known. No instant alterations occur, but a gradual and growing confidence in love's understanding and fidelity will enable more creativity and emotional freedom to emerge. A gradual process of exploring the origins of our emotional habits will emerge. Perhaps one of us may have had a parent who complained too much. Therefore we dare not express any frustration because we have identified with the other parent who always solved the problem. Perhaps one of us learned to strongly express disappointment as the only means of asserting any self-identity in relation to a more dominating partner who never acknowledged any weakness or problems. An inherited unholy balance of opposites needs to give way to an exploration of differences and their family origins, so an intimacy of mutual sharing emerges and replaces the dreaded silence barriers or the arsenal of attacks launched to break down those barriers. In this retuning and listening process, marriage becomes a playful work of maturing persons exploring together past models of problem-solving, creating new ways forward, neither demonizing nor beatifying previous models, and learning how to re-negotiate the impasses we have inherited.

The help that creates nurturing space to grow ceases blaming and accusing. Instead we learn to become friendly towards process, not impatient. It is no crime for this evolving communion of two-become-one to take time to develop and to stumble and fall as we learn to stand, to walk, to run. There is no hurry to become Mr and Mrs Mature and miss the pleasure of the journey into maturity. The first faltering steps of a non-condemning dialogue after many fruitless falls into silence or accusation are to be savoured like the first steps of a child.

Consider the way of our Lord, how he came to help, how he came as Saviour. He came as a baby, not as the omnipotent, omniscient, omnipresent Father. He learned through what he suffered. We have been given the clearest sacramental sign that the process of growing with its stumbles and falls is not to be despised. We make mistakes. But then we may offer and receive the good and humbling gift of forgiveness, as we mutually learn to respect one another's differing burdens, hurts, goals–supporting not solving. Wife and husband say to one another: 'I'm just a sinner who loves you and promises to be alongside you . . . not superior, not inferior.' By the mutual grace of agape we venture together into the love of God which allows sinners, not ideal people, to embrace and to go on pilgrimage.

For many of us, the call to discipleship occurs within the vulnerable vessel of marriage, which nonetheless becomes the safe container that helps us grow into the God-inscribed image carved into our very flesh, this creative, mutual giving and receiving of love. With gladness we rejoice in God's presence in the calm sailing, and with a prayer for courage, we endure and navigate the storms, even negotiating the occasional sea-serpent. But it is the cruciform healing of forgiveness that makes the marriage craft flexible, unadorned, and strong enough to anchor safely in the most precarious ports that life presents. In openness and honesty, we together share in trials and tribulations hopeful in the knowledge that whatever the darkest Good Fridays we share together, Easter is coming. In humility we confess that we do not turn the sky from darkness to light, but God does.

And so with this faith in Love's faithfulness, we learn in our measure to be faithful in our work and comforted in our play as we evolve our own suitable rhythm of work and leisure within a friendship of creative exploration. In the practice of prayer we learn how to interpret and explore the meaning of our discouragements, our dreams, and our desires. Meanwhile, throughout the voyage, our anchor is the realism of a love that reaches out of heaven's perfection to embrace sinners in Jesus of Nazareth. He is the one who turns the waters of human hope and weakness into the forgiving, enabling wine of the kingdom of God.

5

A Gathering of Sinners

Because God's love reaches out from heaven's perfection to embrace the soiled people of earth, families are not abandoned to their imbalances and fears. To recall a biblical analogy, the church is a potter's workshop whose furnishings consist largely of a shaping-wheel and all manner of awkward lumps of clay, some broken, some misshapen, which are in various shapes of transformation. As the potter works the clay in his hands, the imperfections within the clay come to the surface. These are broken, strengthened, and remoulded *in his hands.* Such activity may seem a bit out of place if church is meant to be a display gallery of idealized spiritual portraits, but it is quite appropriate in the workshop of the potter who patiently works his own creative and healing patterns into our lives. For those with eyes to see, not even the most splintered fragments are wasted.

If God chooses to work with such materials in a personal 'hands on' way, it makes no sense to blame and shame the clay for being in process of formation. What did we expect in a potter's house? Within the workshop, the rubble and fragments are being formed into treasure. Let us examine some of the fragments and fears brought to the workshop which is the Church.

Repeating Childhood Patterns

Projecting and Absorbing

Adrift in a flotsam and jetsam of advice, disapproval, and complaint swirling in his mind, a drowning minister cries out: 'If only I had a more worthy congregation, I could grow and mature into a truly loving leader.' Another cleric living at the opposite pole of reaction, blames not the flock, but the shepherd: 'If only I was a more gifted and able minister, these people would be happily maturing.' The congregation has its own version of this pattern as has been recorded in a satirical chain-letter which arrives in the church post: 'If you are unhappy with your present vicar simply have your church secretary send a copy of this letter to six other churches who are tired of their vicar. Then bundle up your vicar and send him to the church at the top of the list in this letter. Within a week you will receive 1,435 vicars and one of them should be all right. Have faith in this chain-letter for vicars. Do not break the chain. One church did and got their old vicar back.' In previous generations, the Church more commonly played the role of the 'blamee', and felt increasingly condemned and guilty for failing to live up to the 'gospel'. Pastor and people need to discover skills in respecting criticism, neither swallowing nor spewing it out. Once the temperature calms down, the patterns of conflict can be explored in non-blaming, mutually supportive ways. Critics can begin to use their criticisms as windows into their own souls, not that of others. Our responses to criticism become windows into our own state of mind and heart. As in marriage, so here, one side may discover why we are never free to acknowledge our frustrations or disappointments, while the other may explore the compulsion to express each rather thoroughly.

Perhaps we experience a huge reaction to a particular critical comment. We say something we regret or we carry it around pounding at us for the next week. What does this inner anguish signify? It tells us that we are immersed in a last straw reaction. The haystack may have been growing since early childhood. There is no relief from the surface wound until, with a trusted friend or counsellor in a time of confession, we drain the abscess down below where the real pressure resides.

Helpers and Helpees

What happens when helpers and helpees venture into church, seeking intimacy with God? A helper's conversion is nearly identical with becoming 'in charge', and taking on leadership. He is called to preach, to be a pillar of the community. Problems emerge, however, when the helper-convert so busily denies himself and keeps busy 'doing things for Jesus' that he howls like Peter when Jesus kneels to wash his feet. He has not the time, he does not know how, to receive ministry, to be prayed for (it is humiliating), to sit at Jesus' feet as a Mary, to openly depart from the clamorous crowds to be in stillness before the Father in refreshment and renewal: 'That kind of receptivity is a luxury I cannot afford when so many people need my help.'

Because direct receptivity is undeveloped or unacceptable, the helper-convert develops an indirect way to receive secret pay-offs: extracting praise by being a model of commitment, being constantly needed and noticed, the centre of attention. Tragically, as a last resort and hidden cry for help when these pay-offs are insufficient, he may become enmeshed in a dishonest or addictive relationship, with a substance or a person. Albert Camus has exposed the grandiosity hidden within the helper's generosity and graphically depicted how 'too many people now climb onto the cross merely to be seen from a greater distance, even if they have to trample somewhat on the one who has been there so long'.[1] A devout Christian life or a 'lively church' certainly appear to be places of self-emptying and serving. That ingredient is undoubtedly there somewhere, but there is also the ingredient of performance: trying to make a good impression, trying to please or win God's affection or my congregation's approval. To the extent these ingredients remain hidden and untouched by the Potter, they become corrosive. Our care-giving becomes unsupported and unsound. Sooner or later doubters and critics raise distressing dissonant noises. Never quite certain our effort is good enough, we press harder. We become candidates for envy and rivalry toward other 'helpers'. Meanwhile from my lofty perch of charity, I cannot help but resent the little brother whose shoes I metaphorically must still tie, or the spiritually immature whose dinner I must fix, and thus I cannot but scold as I serve and complain as I care. This is the church/family love which many of us are too familiar with receiving and dispensing. It is not so much healing intimacy as anxious intensity which wearies the soul of giver and receiver. Saul of Tarsus was a helper.

The Prodigal Helpee

What happens when the overbalanced receiver, the 'helpee', responds to God and returns to church? When I am overbalanced on the receptivity side, I come to church to have God take my problems away. I have acquired a filter through which I hear the church (helper) saying: 'To experience love is to have your needs met.' I am invited to trust this ministry, to allow it to interpret the Bible for me, pray for me, entertain and inspire me, and all shall be well. I do not chew and digest the truth for myself. I am willingly seduced into becoming a spiritual spectator, fascinated by the godly gifts and ascetic acrobatics of the official helpers.

Can you see how a chronic helper and a chronic receiver perpetuate an unhealthy balancing act? It is as if the nominal and needy provide a necessary counterweight to the overworked and zealously conscientious. Like two drunks who stagger into each other, resentfully propping up each other in a mutual spiritual stupor, the compulsive carer rather desperately finds his balance by attaching himself to the very needy. All goes well for a time, until the devout get fed up with the lack of positive change, repentance, and then in frustration change their tactics by exhorting the helpee to measure up: 'You are being foolish not to feel gratitude', 'You must pull yourself together', 'You have no right to feel angry', 'You ought to enjoy helping those less fortunate than yourself'. Upon receiving such 'help' the helpee either storms out or gradually distances and moves on to more sympathetic pastures. Sometimes Mother Church or the con-scientious leader in great frustration can be heard muttering: 'I prayed for you, worshipped for you, taught you, comforted you, advised you, and now you are not coming anymore. What ingratitude!' Maybe the errant pew fodder has been sitting down wearily at St Murgatroyd's-down-the-lane or jumping joyfully in the aisles at St Lively's. Do they have more to give over there? Perhaps there is a fresh supply of care-givers from which one can feed off. Perhaps one can find some much needed space to have a rest from all the anxious attention. Perhaps they are bone weary of the glib advice which flows unself-critically like a never ending stream of platitudes. Meanwhile, the weary helper may find himself searching for a flock with fewer awkward sheep to care for or in exhaustion simply stays home to lick his wounds. Of course none of us are pure 'helpers' or 'helpees', but when we feel insecure or under pressure, we revert to type and become stuck in the old unredemptive patterns in our churches as in our homes.

Dominance and Submission

Frequently a particularly painful childhood wound is unknow-ingly revisited in church life. A child dwells in the house of a weak mother and a dominating father. Early on a decision is made never to undergo such humiliation at the bottom of a pile and so she identifies with the one who rules the roost. As an adult disciple, this person continually relates within a domineering, parental role in all church assignments. If she is not in charge, the programme is unorganized. Co-operation means doing it her way. Ironically, to have her way, she will draw on the weakness of tears and sentimentality to succeed. Not to be at the centre or in control or giving help to the needy is to be left before the ancient wound of fear of abandonment and rejection, despised as weak and useless. Until this childhood wound is faced, the victims become the victimizers of others, and by their tyrannical tendencies live near the edge of being persecuted or abandoned by their new families, the very threat so heavily defended against by their dominating strategy. Until the fear, the hurt, and the strategy are acknowledged with friends or a pastor who can create a safe environment, committed to love and believing that the truth sets us free, the painful pattern internalized in childhood continues unabated. But how often do we find a group both tough enough to face and name the twisted pattern and tender enough to support the victim hidden beneath the aggressive behaviour? Too many churches suffer the debilitating consequences of a dominating vicar, elder or deacon who uses the congregation in this way. The quarrel is extended. Sides are drawn. This unofficial war suffers many casualties, and the church's energies for service are depleted.

There are many variants on this theme of domination and resistance to submission. Doctrines and all manner of good causes are drawn in. We may as easily use orthodoxy or progressive teachings as the cause for the mounting of a holy war against selected sinners whose aberration must be challenged, for the sake of the kingdom. Rather than agreeing with our adversary quickly (Matt. 5.25), the fighter for dominance prefers conflict, is even energized by it, and may even enjoy litigation, the more public, the better.

The very thought of acknowledging and accepting weakness instead of avoiding, denying, or condemning sends emergency alert sirens sounding throughout an inner system in which the dominance and submission, strength and weakness dichotomy is engrained in our souls. Should, in the course of Bible study, a weakness, a confession of sin, hurt or unbelief dare be confessed, quickly it is met with tales of success and victory. There is no mutual weeping. That is too painful and scary. Why allow the Holy Spirit in stillness to touch the opened wound, surround it with the quiet acceptance of respect, when I can rush in and remind the group that I once had a problem like that and it is, essentially and with all due humility, gone now, praise the Lord? Hidden in my anxiety to care, to solve my neighbour's weakness, and to talk the strong talk, is my own fear of weakness and being out of control. I use my strong talk to subtly shame unbelief and drive it underground where it belongs, where my own unbelief and weakness has been driven by the good intentions of my teachers and pastors who also were too frightened by the leprosy of weakness to embrace it.

There is also a more quiet, inward struggle with the consequences of impingement and domination. An earnest seeker searching for healing exhausts the resources of charismatic prayer groups and trained psychotherapists alike. The victim feels locked in prison. When hopeless, suicide seems the only way out. When energized by anger, the prisoner rattles the cage by challenging the system, attacking the status quo, and the competence or sincerity of the legion of advisers. The result of this oscillating strategy–noisy, despairing cry against the collective jailors followed by hopeless helplessness–is that each helper in turn feels inadequate, a failed daddy, an uncaring mum. Frustrated by our failed rescue attempts, it is tempting to blame the victim, and to send him away as lacking faith, as being lazy, as enjoying his prison, as preferring to destroy instead of to build.

However, what if we permit ourselves the cruciform experience of bearing the pain? We discover that what has been shared but so far rejected by the care-groups and helpers are feelings of hopelessness, failure, and incompetence, mingled with anger and hurt; the very feelings the wounded adult felt as a child before unempathic parents or siblings. These are the feelings we now feel having tried unsuccessfully to help and to intervene. Rather than defend ourselves against this painful message or blame the messenger, we may receive it and bear it for a little while in small measure, grieving our own feelings of inadequacy and uselessness. As we listen to our pain, we may discover the clue which reveals the unidentified wound of our client, which the victim has borne alone from childhood. At last the message and the wound and the victim are heard. The victim is not blamed nor is his problem solved by my good advice or by my heroic rescue, with all its potential for romantic grandiosity. Instead we share in a small way the pain of being made to feel incompetent and useless which the victim has felt for a lifetime. We weep with those who weep. But I can only do this when my hungering need to cure, to control, to succeed is named and sacrificed, in a mutual experience of my limits and God's mercy within the brokenness of our human story. Healing in its proper measure comes to both care-giver and care-receiver through an unexpected path as old as the proud Roman cross dominating the skyline of Jerusalem, with its threats and punishment and curse, yet sowing a new seed of dominion in place of domination, a new form of power, bearing it into the very heart of the old diseased system, at the very place of shame and humiliation. As the echo of Calvary's mystery touches my life, Easter gently rises in me.

Religious Abuse

A parent who threatens to withhold love in order to compel submission, creates an anxious clinging to the very parent who so threatens us. A child who has been sexually abused, who has only experienced exploitative caresses, has no choice but to accept any closeness she is offered. There is even a repetitive compulsion to search out the same kind of unsatisfying love. An addictive substance, for example, whiskey, cigarettes, food, or a sex-object, hooks us by providing a temporary feeling of comfort like an available nurturing parent gives, while also providing the torments of dependency and built-in inadequacy, the very kind of anguished attachment we once had at home. There is a religious equivalent.

The very god who frightens us, we long for and cling to, for fear of abandonment. The roots of the fundamentalist god's authority by power and threat can be found in a childhood where might makes right: 'Don't ask why. That's disrespectful. Do as you're told. Do it now!' One child brought up in a home where a parent threatens rejection, or suicide, is strangely drawn to a preacher who motivates us to stay on the right path by repeated hints, or bald threats, of punishment. We are once again enthralled by a god who we desperately need but who offers no guarantees of love. Our being loved, our salvation is always conditional upon our faithfulness, not God's. And so the very heart of biblical faith is turned upside down. Meanwhile, the other child plays the role of rebel and becomes the village atheist disbelieving in such a god. Whether anxiously attached or anxiously rebelling and hating, both are enthralled by this foreboding god of conditional love. We are preoccupied with our 'personal salvation' and have little or no energy left to toil in the kingdom. We do unto others the same 'threatening love' which has been done unto us. We compete for or lash out against this limited and conditional love. Whereas a word of warning springs from love, for example, 'Don't touch that plate, it's hot. I love you and don't want you to be hurt', a threat implies an equal pleasure in punishment as in reward, such as the god satirized in Burns's poem, 'Holy Willie's Prayer', who sends 'ane to heaven and ane to hell, all for God's glory'.

The appeal of a cult hooks into this deep inner confusion. In a moment of emptiness and grief, I hear a guru or an idealized leader tell me that if I will trust him, his church will teach me the true meaning of the Gospel. Perhaps I hear some fresh examples of love and sacrifice. Temporarily I abandon my self-centredness to embrace the inspired leader or group as my new centre. I experience relief from the pain of my inner parents' conditional love. I find an ideal nurturing mother in the group. All seems well as long as I sacrifice and obey. Then one day something in me once again tests the boundaries. I raise too many questions, express a doubt, or become ill. I become increasingly suspect. Gradually I sense that the idealized group mother mercilessly requires the same adaptation to its demands that my real parents once did. Dare I rebel, I face the same threats, but this time with eternal repercussions. The Church as cult intimidates in the same old way. I cling with the same deep fear of abandonment. I am strangely at home in a familiar prison, for a while.

Of course the Church is not the only group that can function as an abusive parent. I may be emotionally vulnerable to the latest 'ideal group'. Political parties and ideologies may hook in to my anxious attachment to a parental protective system, which rewards unquestioned obedience, and forbids questioning of authority on threat of abandonment. The penchant to replace one bad parent with a group or a substance or a theory in this addictive way is perpetual until we are given permission to begin a process of mourning what we have lost or never received. Recurrent religious conversions or denominational transfers–

temporary attachments followed by disappointment and detachment–habitually perpetuate the loss by repeating it, not grieving it. To leave the group without replacing it with another anxious attachment creates a hideous loneliness and guilt. Soon even more terrible gods replace the vacuum of aloneness that nature abhors. No wonder a fierce atheism or cold indifference is chosen by some to defend them from further assault. Nonetheless a totalitarian lover lives on in my inner life. His domain is permanent unless I find a lover who does not call me to submit, but comes to give his life on my behalf in sheer grace. Only then I am free to discover a new world with a new kind of authority, under the dominion of the servant king. Only He shall reign for ever and ever.

The Eros Community

We have seen how early on in a marriage or in romantic love, we attach ourselves to others because they meet our needs and we find them attractive. Gradually we allow the other space and freedom to be themselves and value them even when they do not make us feel wanted and attractive or when we do not find them desirable. Similarly we tend to idealize the new church we have joined in a way which parallels the romantic projection of my paper doll. But after a few committee meetings, a few times feeling ignored, or sensing how that sermon with a political edge creates a surprising amount of acrimony, I discover the wounded egos and the very human rivalries which lurk among the pews and pulpit. Shall I leave disappointed in search for a more lovely bride of Christ? Next time shall I find one which asks nothing but for me to be consistent pew fodder? Bonhoeffer wisely counsels that this disillusioning process is an essential part of community growth. 'Only the fellowship which faces such disillusionment, with all its unhappy and ugly aspects, begins to be what it should be in God's sight, begins to grasp in faith the promise that is given to it . . . He who loves his dream of a community more than the Christian community itself becomes a destroyer of the latter, even though his personal intentions may be ever so honest and sacrificial.'[2]

When pastors and leaders are gravely overbalanced in care-giving, to the point of being 'helpaholics', disillusionment is a frequent spiritual infection. After trying so hard, to see numbers fade or programmes die or critics rise up or an endless repetition of duties with no relief, creates an acute experience of failure and weariness. Increasingly anxious to succeed, we redouble our efforts. But eventually, we have nothing left to give. Only then do we face the radical nature of our limits. This is a painful encounter. To have this grand vision of being that special kind of leader who would make all the difference in a community, and now to see it lie in shambles as there seems more dissension or more nominalism than ever after all our toil.

This letting go of our wish-dream of finding or forging the ideal community is necessary for refining and clarifying our faith in the Gospel, for my faith was never meant to rest upon the collective spirituality of an ideal flock, but rather in the merciful and holy God who eats and drinks at a common table with sinners. As Robert Stamps's communion hymn puts it so powerfully, prophets, patriarchs, angels, and elders are not the only ones who gather round to celebrate and bear witness that God meets us in the lowly holiness of mercy: 'Beggars, lame and harlots also here. Repentant publicans are drawing near. Wayward sons come home without a fear. God and man at Table are sat down.'[3]

Idealizing a group disappoints as surely as idealizing a romantic partner. We put impossible expectations on the Church to make us happy or fulfilled. We may even cope with our romantic disappointment at home by projecting it onto the Church and quarrel with the bride of Christ rather than our own bride. The sheer realities of budgets, buildings, emotional differences, and imbalances from our past systems, eventually cause our wish-dream community to break down. I am faced with becoming a member of the real body of which I am another awkward part. As my wish-dream experiences crucifixion, finally I may be ready to step deeper into love's labour and reward in the community. If not, I am destined to repeat the process one more time, that is, if in my hunger and loneliness, I risk being disappointed one more time. Churches, like humans, are often immature lovers, seeking self, breaking promises, abandoning, rejecting, impinging. These folk are definitely not ideal lovers we are bound to in the Church. Discovering our solidarity in sin is a crucial step in finding our true focus and hope for a deeper life together.

The fact is that we gather to worship not in an ideal setting, with all manner of ideal brothers and sisters, but we gather in the church, a hospital ward for sinners, not a sanitized hotel for saints; a potter's workshop, not an art gallery. By grace it becomes for us a place to discover and recover the meaning of our lives in the Gospel and lay bare the bagful of wish-dreams, our blaming games, our inflated and deflated predispositions–all symptoms of hate, fear, and self-absorption which need healing. By grace the church becomes a safe place to bring our whole selves, wounds and gifts, sorrows and joys, in an atmosphere of God's cleansing judgement and mercy. In such a place, we can discover salvation and healing not as a magic cure but as the untwisting of our disfigured hearts and minds.

In Romans chapter twelve, St Paul describes the way love expresses itself in Christian community. Here we see tears are as welcome as laughter; fears and doubts may be honestly acknowledged and not hushed up. We discover harmony not competitive rivalry. We are committed to forgiveness, not revenge. We bless those who persecute us. We pursue equality, rejecting the pride of superiority and the hidden pride of inferiority. The love of God builds a community which reflects God's own interior character. This is why a community of faith is a place where wounds are healed, resentments forgiven, old resistant habits overcome, and fears are replaced with hopes.

Lessons from the Wilderness

But Rome was not built in a day and neither is a community of love. Israel's journey to the promised land, and its struggle to be God's people uniquely exposes some of the structural resistances and road-blocks to community which must be overcome. Informed by the work of Wilfrid Bion on task-avoiding behaviours, recent projects including Scott Peck's Community Building Workshops and Jean Vanier's L'arche Communities have explored the dynamics of group resistances to a healthy community.[4] The children of Israel's own story helps us to appreciate how deeply embedded these resistances are and also helps us see real hope for overcoming them.

The Golden Calf Crisis: Exodus 32

It is worth remembering that Israel is a community born out of crisis. Her rescue shows signs that the hard times which knit the people together during their escape, are insufficient to develop them further as a community once the external enemy is eliminated. The flood-waters of outer rescue have barely receded than the murmuring begins at the Springs of Elim. Disenchantment with their basic provisions of living arises. Manna is fair enough at first, but they soon miss their Egyptian (flesh)pot-luck dinners. Moses goes away on a sabbatical to Mount Sinai and leaves the people with Aaron and more autonomy than a slave mentality can manage. Moses is in transition from ruling the people by personal charisma to himself standing under the covenant and guidance of God, which he is receiving up on the mountain of transcendence. But the people are impatient and fearful. Their anxious worship culminates in the golden calf.

The calf quickly papers over the cracks of their lack of common purpose. Perhaps like the United States without the threat of the Soviet Union, the Hebrews are searching for a common project to bind them together. Not a dominating Pharaoh, Moses withdraws as Jesus does later from a clamoring crowd, to listen to God. As their wish-dream begins to fade, the people begin the strategy of blame the leader and complain. Moses is slow of speech. He is not a good planner. The manna seems a last minute solution. The only community they have ever known is a dominance–submission model. Away on the mountain Moses is preparing for something new. But the people seek to rescue their ideal by projecting it onto a glittering external project.

Remember, there are two ways to be enslaved. One way is the Pharaoh-totalitarian way, such as was Eastern Europe until recently. This is the slavery described by George Orwell's *1984*. This 'obey or else' way creates at once resentment and dependency. But there is also the operant-conditioning way of enslavement described by Aldous Huxley's *Brave New World* where because one is addicted to stimulants and pleasures, continually reinforced by easy accessibility, we are willing victims, conditioned to tune in, turn on, consume and be moulded. Big Brother does not watch over and control us. By our conditioning and addiction to amusement we choose to willingly watch what Big Brother wants us to see.[5] The goal of politics and religion is to make us comfortable and fulfil our expectations. In freedom from external control, we are now susceptible to having a god who will be immanently accessible, not away on Mount Sinai, behind clouds of unknowing and repentance. There is a passion

for a god who is a good show, who dazzles, someone who celebrates our own creativity and giftedness. The gold flows, the
orgy begins as the people celebrate their victory, their talents,
and strength, now epitomized by the beautiful, powerful,
sleek bull of gold. This religious and political captivity emerges
from within our hearts and is not imposed from without. We are
enthralled by a god of garish power and splendour. Meanwhile,
away in the distance, the silence, the wilderness, above the cloud
and smoke of Mount Sinai, the covenant God of holiness and mercy
encounters Moses personally, unveiling his will and character.

The wish-dream for an ideal leader seduces Israel to blame
Moses. His God is too invisible, at once too distant and too imma-
nent. The dominance-submission habit causes Israel to willingly
wish to be overwhelmed by its golden god as once Pharaoh dominated her externally. Aaron, anxious to rescue, finds a fast way
to make the people happy and bring control to the chaos. Thank
goodness for Aaron, a man with the common touch, who can
bring us a god who will ensure our success, help us regain control. Out of our fears we cry: 'Aaron, bring us god!' And the
people are willing to pay large amounts of gold and silver for this
splendid, awesome god born of their own creativity, fears and
hungers. Like so many after him, Aaron only causes more hurt
and chaos by his efforts to fix it for Israel. His anxious attempt to
help is profoundly unhelpful.

The bad news is that when we fabricate a god of convenience
and attraction out of our needs and fears, this god is probably a
golden calf. The true God remains beyond our control, beyond
our wish-dreams, on Mount Sinai. But the good news is that this
Lord is a lover with everlasting faithfulness so deep he interrupts
our worship of idols even though it means disappointment. It is
painful to abandon false gods and to face the extent of our distance from the truth which we tried to smooth over with our
golden bull.

Feeling the emptiness where formerly stood our secure and
confident idol, God seems very absent and we feel broken and
hopeless without our ideal. But the experience of God's absence
is basic to biblical faith. Israel must first disbelieve in all her
imaged and projected deities before she is free to believe in the
God who will be known by personal acquaintance as in intimacy
he tells us his name and discloses his character. In the New
Testament the generic messianic expectations must be laid aside

so that Jesus can reveal himself to us as he is, not as we expect him to be. So God is first concealed by the cross, its pain and suffering, before He is revealed on the cross. So Jesus Christ himself crying out from the depths, despairs with the despairing and intercedes on our behalf. Faith sees his cry of dereliction as the assurance of his presence in the cross, coming alongside us, but only as our golden calves and messianic expectations, military conqueror or magician, are melted down. In his prayer for God to take his life rather than destroy Israel (Exod. 32.30–2), Moses' willingness to sacrifice himself, not to dominate or solve her problems, introduces the way of emptying in which alone a community may grow. Moses lets go of his unfulfilled wishes, and lays them sacrificially before God, in intercession, not cursing disobedient Israel, but seeking to bless. Separating out his own false desire for heroics from his willingness to sacrifice his own role for the sake of the community, Moses sees the promised land from a distance, and leads in this new, unheroic way. The inner life of contemporary leaders shall also experience the refiner's fire, burning away the wood, hay, and stubble of our motivations, in order that non-perishable treasures emerge.

Temptation to Flight

In Numbers 13 and 14 we read of Moses telling the people to be of good courage and, unlike him, they shall enter the promised land. But with the exception of Joshua and Caleb, the other ten spies' fears are greater than their desires: 'We can't do it.' And we too are masters of avoidant strategies. Many of our addictive behaviours stem from a basic flight from the pain and the problem implicit in the task to which we are called. We may use alcohol or ceaseless activity to avoid the pain of relationships and tasks that are not working. For all its healthy common sense, even the strategy of positive thinking can simply be a cover-up for the fear of failure, the fear of acknowledging a tragic situation for which the cross is the only honest remedy. Success stories of rejoicing are repeated like mantras rather than having to endure the pain of weeping and confronting our loss.

Clandestine or blatant, the enticement to flight reaches to the heart of what faith in Jesus means. Did Jesus only appear to come as a human? Was he really in all points tempted as we are? Were his cries on the cross truly agony or merely perfor-

mance? Was Jesus only a figure of heavenly light who never
knew death or was he indeed a man of sorrows acquainted with
grief? Does he redeem only light or did he actually 'descend
into hell'? Can hell be redeemed or just avoided? The pain we
hide or run from drains our energy and creativity. We overwork
in keeping away from the dangers. By contrast, biblical faith
faces the darkness and the dangers. It is reality based, not ideal
based.

The perennial popularity of 'positive thinking' reminds us that
positive feelings are an essential part of healing. But negative
feelings are important also. They are usually the clue leading
us to the source of the wound which must be resolved, not
buried alive. Love casts out fear rather than steers clear of it. A
Christian community faces the tragic side of life because Jesus
did not avoid his enemies, but embraced them on the cross.

Temptation to Fight: Numbers 16.1–4

Instead of kneeling with hoe, sweating with honest labour, we
may argue about how to organize the cultivation. Korah was a
very gifted leader, sensitive to the people's needs, who skilfully
organized the people. But unlike Moses' father-in-law, he uses his
gifts to fight Moses, not to work alongside. He impugns Moses'
motives, undermines confidence, and tries to distance Moses
from the people by accentuating his differences. In Luke 12, a
man seeks to draw Jesus into a property dispute and have him
fight on his side. But Jesus refuses to play judge at a small claims
court set up by our greed. Instead Jesus encourages the one
crying for his fair share to look for the deeper motive. This
man's task is not to score a victory over his brother in court, but
to discover who he really is. Another unwelcome Messianic
answer? There are more. In John 5 an adulterous woman is
brought to Jesus. Whose side will Jesus support? He replies that
she is a scapegoat, that the people's true dilemma is not the
woman, but the desire to blame her, punish her, while their
own sins remain unconfessed. 'Let him who is without sin cast
the first stone.' To the woman, he does not say, 'I'm on your
side'. He tells her that her deepest problem is not her accusers,
but her own passion misplaced in self-destructive relationships:
'Go and sin no more.'

It is tempting to fight with our enemies instead of 'agreeing with them quickly', honouring them, or learning from them. Mohammad chose to fight. When he conquered Mecca, he descended upon it with his horsemen and put his enemies to the sword. But Jesus neither flees for safety–he sets his face like steel towards Jerusalem–nor does he fight. The 10,000 legions of angels remain bemused in their barracks. His conflict reaches to a profounder level, through atonement. The cross is his conclusive entry into the depths of our complaints and quarrels. And there he engages us not to judge and condemn, but to judge in order to heal. Atonement is his healing alternative to fighting, but not a cheap or easy one.

Pairing: The Tragedy of Rehoboam, 1 Kings 12.

The story of Solomon's succession records how the United Kingdom became torn into the northern and the southern tribes. As a result, first the north and then the south are taken into captivity. How did this occur? By identifying exclusively with the advice of the young and ignoring the counsel of the old, Rehoboam, son of Solomon, alienates the north. The young see only the importance of raising taxes further to add to the splendours of the king and his court. The old are weary of these tax and spend policies, which create grand expressions of power but leave the people with little for themselves. Rehoboam decides not to reach a consensus, but to overwhelm his opponents and send them packing.

The Church's equivalent would be for the eye to say to the hand, 'I have no need of thee'. In small groups two folk begin whispering while another, making herself vulnerable, is sharing a personal word. The others sense this is not a safe place to bring the real self behind the public persona. Others will not listen. They may laugh.

Sometimes groups pair-off by arguing over styles of worship or music. We become specialists in what Lewis's Screwtape calls 'Christianity and . . . healing, socialism, conservatism, spelling reform'.[6] We avoid the task of mission by pairing-off into special identity groups, waging war for our alliance, not feeding the sheep or searching for lost sheep. We are proud to be Evangelical Christians, Charismatic Christians, Progressive Christians, High Church, Low Church, House Church, not 'mere' Christians. The antidote occurs when we recover the richness of the body's diversity and are grateful for hands, eyes, feet, and various appendages as being integral parts of the body of Christ.

Alliances spring from fear and the hope to retain power. But each time the young and the old permit their different strengths to work together, joy erupts as the whole is experienced under the one head which is Christ. Community deepens and widens. There is healing each time a Peter who has stopped eating with gentile believers is called by a Paul to sit at the table again, for Jesus their mutual Lord has knit together gentile and Jew on the cross.

It is Jesus himself who knits together the north and south of Israel in his own person. Born in the south, raised in the north, he tells the south of a northern Samaritan who is a neighbour to the southerner in danger. He himself is at once the son of man, and son of God, at all points tempted as we are, yet the very God who never snatches at deity, but empties himself to heal by holy love.

> For he is our peace, who has made us both one, and has broken down the dividing wall of hostility, by abolishing in his flesh the law of commandments and ordinances, that he might create in himself one new man in place of the two, so making peace, and might reconcile us both to God in one body through the cross, thereby bringing the hostility to an end. And he came and preached peace to you who were far off and peace to those who were near; for through him we both have access in one Spirit to the Father. (Eph. 2.14–18)

The Dependency Tendency: I Samuel 8

Samuel, the judge of Israel, is growing old, and his sons are not up to the task of taking on leadership. The people want a king like the other nations 'who will fight our battles for us'. Here lies exposed the subtle collusion between a dominant leader and a subject people. The people are 'taken care of' more or less (usually less) and they do not have to take responsibility for their own maturity. King Saul, like many a gifted person after him, is inflated at the thought of being a strong leader and tries very hard to successfully use his ample natural abilities. Despite the odd success, he becomes increasingly unpopular and ends a failure. Whenever a group is too dependent on one leader to solve its problems, a backlash insures that the exalted leader is brought down to earth. Like Saul, some of us are spiritually egotistical enough to fall into this trap. Like Israel, many of us are willing to transfer responsibility for our maturity to someone else, and then to blame them when it does not work. So Israel lifts Saul on a pedestal, and when he falls, he is blamed without mercy. That is, except for David, who spares his life and honours his family even after Saul's death. Many churches suffer from a dependency tendency, putting a priest on a pedestal, and blaming him when he falls from the heights.

It is this same thirst to have someone take care of us, to have someone fight our battles for us, that causes Israel to reject Jesus as their Messiah. Unlike Saul, Jesus refuses what most leaders are too egotistical to decline, namely, letting the people write his job description. If Saul angers the people as a failed king, how much more does Jesus's refusal to be their sort of Messiah infuriate those whose expectations he disappoints. Jesus is not the Messiah who overwhelms his opponents and dazzles his people by magically leaping unhurt from the pinnacle of the temple or turning stones into bread. He refuses the nationalistic expectations to throw off Caesar's yoke. Jesus's concern is with a far profounder bondage. So he heals spontaneously along the road rather than orchestrated in an amphitheatre. But the dependency tendency wants a messianic breakthrough straight-away by force, not as a seed growing secretly, dying and then rising.

Jesus is the Messiah who disappoints our dependent wish-dream for a hero. He is instead a pilgrim, who will himself become perfect through his sufferings (Heb. 5.8). Dependency misunderstands grace to mean that because God works, we are idle. Dependency assumes that 'grace alone' means 'grace in solitude'. But grace grants us freedom to work and believe all the more (1 Cor. 15.10). Paul calls us co-workers, not passive specta-tors. Too often we who lead the Church have so enjoyed being 'in charge' and centre-stage, we collude with the congregation's preference for passive recipiency. In spite of our exhaustion, we muffle the theme of the priesthood of all believers, that we are to be a nation of priests, lest credit, attention, and power be distributed too broadly.

Here too the outmoded model of healing from medicine, where we have an active doctor and a passive patient, retains too much influence and is an exceedingly limited model of healing.

How different from a passive patient is a disciple of the Servant Lord who is called to go on a pilgrimage in his steps. The Lord of the journey is not someone who suffers so we do not, but as George MacDonald reminds us, he suffers in order that our suffering may be like his. Our unbalanced patterns and romantic expectations are unhelpful baggage pilgrims must shed in order to be fit and lean for the journey. The difficulties of the journey are substantial. But our help is the Lord of pilgrims, who accompanies us in order to create disciples, not dependency, that we would be of good courage as we negotiate deep valleys and high mountains.

Perhaps there is no steeper ascent and no greater opportunity to plummet in error than when love dares to enter the political fray. But if love has a mandate to impact community life and is not the private domain of individual behaviour only, this road too must be travelled.

Notes

1   Albert Camus, *The Fall*, (Random House, 1956), p. 114.
2   Dietrich Bonhoeffer, *Life Together*, (Harper & Row, 1954), p. 27.
3   Robert Stamps, 'God and Man at Table are Sat Down', *Sounds of Living Water*, (Hodder & Stoughton, 1974), p. 112.
4   cf. Jean Vanier, *Community and Growth*, and M. Scott Peck, *A Different Drum*, (Rider, 1987).
5   cf. Neil Postman, *Amusing Ourselves to Death*, (Penguin, 1985), pp. 137–141.
6   C. S. Lewis, *The Screwtape Letters*, (Collins, [1942], 1971), p. 49.

6

The Politics of Love

A Tale of Two Cities

On 24 August, AD 410, Alaric sacked Rome and pillaged it for three days. The Roman Empire was no more. Shock waves shook the Christian community because since the days of the Emperor Constantine, Christianity had been the official religion of the Roman Empire. Christians feared the end of Rome meant the end of the Church. The enemies of the Church went so far as to blame Christianity for the defeat of the Empire. In the eye of this cultural storm, Augustine wrote *City of God* to interpret the Church's role and the reasons for the fall of Rome. Augustine prophesied that the Church would survive even though the Roman political community might not. Why? Because the political colossus which was Rome was united only by force, not by love. And the gods of Rome that were defeated was not the God of Christians, but the uncivil and destabilizing gods of domination, power and conquest. These had failed the people, and not even making the Christian faith the official religion could paper over the real worship of a society which *de facto* centred its civil order upon these gods. Augustine offered the Christians of his era the vision that all earthly cities are temporary dwellings and that the Christian is a pilgrim whose true citizenship is always the eternal city, the Kingdom of God.

If the loving reign of Jesus Christ relativizes, judges, and redeems all earthly domains, how shall this kingdom which is 'not of this world' affect those outside the community of faith? Does the believer's witness that Christ is the head of the entire human family (Col.1.16–20) come to its end after we (à la Billy Graham) invite individuals to make a personal decision to join the community of Jesus Christ?

The pioneer missionary to Hawaii, Richard Armstrong, concluded that if missionary work begins by proclaiming the Gospel, it must end by organizing society according to the Gospel. Jesus the King of all kings eventually creates a crisis not only for Pontius Pilate, but for all civil rulers. In a letter to his family, Armstrong remarked of the Hawaiians that the 'wretched habits of their former state' could not seem to be shaken off, even though he preached the Gospel and the people embraced it warmly. As a frontline missionary, he thinks he sees why:

> Their government, until recently, was one of the worst forms of despotism, consequently the common people were slaves and could not enjoy either liberty of person or right of property. This state of things cut up all enterprise by the roots, since no man will work for nothing or aim at an object he knows is beyond his reach and in those days a character was formed which will not soon be entirely reformed.[1]

Thus it was that the Gospel-preaching Armstrong soon found himself pleading in the privy council of the king for land reform to give the peasants a stake in their own future, to till their own soil. Meanwhile he continued to build schools throughout the islands so the natives could become literate. The time soon came when he would be invited to become the minister of state for education.

Even prior to the coming of Christian faith to Rome, Augustine reminded the people that the ancients had agreed that a city (*polis* in Greek, from which we derive our word 'political') can grow only so far as religion enlarges its sphere of influence so that larger and larger social groups agree to co-operate. For a city is nothing more nor less than a 'harmonious association of persons'. But the problem with the ancient world, much as with tribalism evident in parts of Africa or in our economically segregated metropolitan areas where a consistent infra-structure of trust and justice has collapsed, is that families, economic tribes, and gangs form a series of closed societies with their own religions and sub-cultures of social order. Natural religion did not say 'this is your brother', but 'this is a stranger. He has other gods'. For larger social groups to grow and co-operate, not compete for power, it was necessary to overcome this separation and distrust between families: 'The religion of gods common to several families alone made possible the birth of the city. Society grew only as fast as religion enlarged its sphere.'[2]

Since the time of Augustine, the desire to connect the vision of the city, or polis, of God, where love is perfected, to the earthly polis, has been a fundamental concern of the Church's mission. Two false roads are clear enough. The first is to identify the temporal church with the city of God and for the Church to play the role of a political power on earth as did the Medieval Church or as did political-religious movements in Nazi Germany (the German Christian's support of Hitler's racial policies) and in modern America (the moral majority's identification with Ronald Reagan), by identifying with one political party, and even one section of that party, of the nation. This temptation to falsely marry spiritual and political power is always recognizable by its exclusivity and self-righteousness. It expresses itself whenever the devout campaign to secure political power for those who avoid selective sins of the flesh (for example, alcohol but not gluttony, homosexuality but not infidelity) while seeking to exclude the civil rights of non-Christians. But whenever we identify the centre of faith with a selective code of ethics, we move to the margins the faithfulness of God's love for all humankind, especially those who are stray and prodigal sheep.

As a consequence, we develop a judgemental attitude to the world, not a cross-centred declaration of God's justification of the sinner. Instead of creating an order based on mercy and justice, a call to repentance based on grace, a religious activism emerges to promote self-righteous confrontation and threat of conquest rather than compassion and the desire to negotiate. It calls for repentance based on threat and intimidation. We must ask, for instance, was this not the difference between the moral crusade of William Wilberforce that ended slavery in the British Empire through parliamentary persuasion and legislation, and the moral crusade of the American Abolitionists from John Brown to Charles Finney that ended in a violent civil war? We must ask whether a certain shrillness of rhetoric and arrogance of moral superiority helped create a climate which ennobled a violent crusade, provoked angry self-justification, and aroused a highly combustible atmosphere in which war was mutually preferable to negotiation. We must ask if this is not the temptation facing the 'moral' black majority in South Africa in its struggle against the racism and vested interests of the minority white population.

The second false road, rather than unequally yoking political and spiritual power, separates the two absolutely by abandoning the earthly polis as a false polis. This way declares the earthly city has nothing to do with a kingdom of love, turns inward and simply focuses on being a good church and hoping for individual salvation for the clan. This way may refuse to pay taxes, refuse to vote, as in Jehovah's Witnesses, or simply refuse to pay attention to the earthly polis. So focused on being a colony of heaven, the Church by neglect and omission builds walls of separation rather than bridges of witness and compassion. In each generation the Church is called to renew itself according to the Gospel. But where this renewal focuses exclusively on the interior care of the congregation, it has forgotten its mandate of mission to the world, to be the Church for the sake of the world.

There are many suggestions that the New Testament has a much more positive attitude toward the earthly polis than this denial but which abstains from an unequal marriage with political power. The 'world' is not simply a demonic city to flee, as if evil has free reign out there and is absent here in church. We are encouraged to pray for all peoples, especially kings and princes (1 Tim. 2.1–7). As a basic part of our debt of love to our neighbour, we are told to pay our taxes to Caesar (Rom.13.7). We are told that the authorities on earth are given their power by the will of God and that their just exercise of these powers matters to God. God cares deeply that rulers promote peace so that the Gospel might be preached to all, because God desires the salvation of all humankind (1 Tim. 2.1–7). That Pontius Pilate was derelict in his duty to protect Jesus and treat him justly infers that he indeed had a proper duty to perform and was remiss.

Most importantly of all, the Church serves the earthly polis when it prophetically proclaims that whether the state knows it or not, Jesus Christ, the king of love, is the Lord of all earthly lords, and that the earthly state is intended to serve the heavenly city through its commitment to being a society which is just, which loves mercy and which walks humbly with God (Mic. 6.8). Part of our obligation to be good subjects of the earthly city (Rom.13.1–7) and to honour the state is by expecting the best of it so it too will serve the Sovereign judge of justice and Author of liberty as it grants and administers liberty and justice.[3] Yes, we are strangers and pilgrims in the earthly city, but at the heart of our faith in the love of Jesus Christ is not only a private hope for individual believers, but a hope for the entire human family and the earthly polis (Eph. 1.10). We desire the state to promote a quiet and peaceable life not merely for our own private happiness that our self-centredness may be undisturbed, but that God's purpose of saving all humankind will be served by a lack of violence and chaos, within a society founded upon the practice and the promise of justice and joy for all the peoples. When we leave the worship service to go to the city hall or the polling booth, we are not passing from Christ's Lordship to another and independent dominion.

A Tale of Two Heresies

When the Church has no prophetic word addressing the love of God to the economic community, we in effect turn the economic life of a city over to the ideological factions of left and right. The ensuing competitors wrestle for economic sovereignty without reference to the larger Lordship of Christ and the Gospel call to create structures that promote and encourage an economic community grounded in love for neighbour and self.

There are two great seductions in the political witness to love in its economic expression. The first is linked to the false marriage between power and religion. I have in mind the communist hijacking of equality and justice by the politics of envy and class-hate that justifies any ruthless means in the name of justice. The essential competitive framework of a class war poisons our moral life as it bears on our economic life. As a result, a hidden envy and jealousy fuels our passion for justice with demonic fires of envy, not the fire of love. The over-arching commitment to equality and the value of the group or whole becomes mutated into the collective totalitarianism of Marxist communism. This de-humanizes by reducing persons, and therefore our humanity, into little cogs of a great economic machine, ruled, as Orwell put it, by those clever pigs who are more equal than the rest of us. Freedom to serve our neighbour is mutated into obedience to the State. The gulag, the concentration camp, and the secret police become characteristic expressions of such a coercive society. This false economy has been astonishingly overturned in recent years. But there is another kind of exploitive society which vitiates the organization of society according to the Gospel. Even now its web is spreading throughout Eastern Europe as communism retreats.

Before we proceed, let us first recall what makes a collection of contiguous families with different gods, as in ancient Rome and modern multi-cultural society's pantheon of ultimate concerns, able to be governed as one city. It is when these different families acquire a religion which enables us to see a stranger as our sister or brother. Only such a group can mutually embrace and learn to make the sacrifices necessary for a harmonious association of persons. As Augustine puts it, in the absence of justice, the authority of any government is little more than organized piracy. Imagine, writes Augustine, two members of a city, one poor, one wealthy. The wealthy man is haunted with fear, heavy with cares, feverish with greed, never secure, always restless and breathless from endless quarrels with his enemies. But by this life-style he adds to his possessions beyond measure. Contrast this with the desperation of the poor. The healing alternative is the serenity of the modest person, who is content with a small, compact patrimony, loved by family, healthy, chaste, and at peace with his conscience. From this context it is clear that for Augustine, a just society, where evil is punished and righteousness is rewarded, entails intentional economic and social components.[4]

So we see that in addition to communism, there is another ideology which the Gospel challenges: a capitalistic individualism whose sole function is profit un-integrated with concern for a just distribution of resources. This is what Karl Barth once called an anarchy from above in which a feverish economic activity is compulsively dictated by competition. It constantly strives to reduce consumer prices in order to maximize profits and so relentlessly expands markets in order to beat my competitor before my competitor beats me. The result is a cycle of over-production, crises, and take-overs with devastating consequences for persons caught in the grip of competition's unregulated feeding frenzy. Even the staunch capitalist Republican, and Quaker-raised, President of the United States, Herbert Hoover, perceived at the time of the Great Depression, that 'the problem with capitalism is capitalists. They're too greedy.' Against this the Christian will explore a way beyond economic egoism towards an economic commitment to a 'harmonious association of persons'.

Without a commitment to economic justice, the peace and stability of a society is under constant threat from this anarchy of the strong or else the rebellion and reprisal from below by the weak. In other words, violence on the streets is begotten by the organized piracy in the city hall and the boardroom. As Robert Bellah remarked following the Los Angeles riots in the summer of 1992, the looting of America did not begin after the Rodney King verdict in Los Angeles, which acquitted the police who brutally beat him. The looting began with the Michael Milkins, the Ivan Boeskys, the Charles Keatings and others who in the 1980s plundered American corporations, financial institutions, and taxpayers on a scale which renders the theft and destabilization in Los Angeles microscopic.

Imagine a family in which the parent owns a stereo and a television, and has good food, but the children are not allowed to use these things because the parent argues they would not appreciate them since they had not earned these themselves. Yet day after day they watch the parents enjoy these things. Rebellion, reprisal, and resistance are inevitable. It is true that if I arrange a sharing and training programme, all these things will wear out faster, and I will have to wait my turn–that is, if I share these with my family and teach them how to use them properly. But a family is more than self-interest. If one is bonded with a family only for convenience or self-development, not love, no family will survive. In order for a city to be governable by mutual harmony not simply by heavily armed police, symptom of an anarchy from above, cities and nations must be fundamentally a family. When one ceases to seek a basic fairness, when the strong and adult no longer seek to train and support the weak and childlike, the family cannot survive, but will, like Rome, eventually be ungovernable, ripe for exploitation by other marauding strangers, whose gods also are domination, power and conquest. Every competent adult was once a child, whose capacity to develop its own latent talents has been essentially due to the support, encouragement and love of the adults and peers who nurtured them.

What can bring together so many different families into a harmonious whole? Both the history of the children of Israel and even more the experience of the early Church suggests a commitment to the fair distribution of goods, education, and medicine is essential in a society in which love is central and not arbitrary. We need not conjure up the old communist spell of an absolute equality in property or means, let alone the revocation of private ownership, but it seems to be a gospel implicate that great surpluses and great shortages are glaring signs of a fundamental absence of justice in any society which tolerates, or whose tax structures create, radical disparities. And again it is the model of Jesus the Lord who came among us as one who served, who 'though he was rich yet for our sakes became poor' that creates a crisis for those who use their freedom, talents, and resources to provide a leadership which maximizes the advantages of the 'adults' while exploiting rather than serving the weak, the childlike, and the children, as do the rulers of the gentiles (Mark 10.42).

The value or even the possibility of life together, 'community life', to which love bears witness is profoundly undercut by the ideology of individualism so pervasive in the West. In individualism, I become the end and my neighbour the means to my self-interest. We honour the individual who is particularly strong or talented. The word 'independent' is used as a developmental goal, with 'dependent' having negative connotations. Love's domain is limited to a private focus on self-happiness, forgetting that our humanity is a co-humanity and love has essentially to do with communion and community. To translate the politics of love merely into my 'human rights' ignores my human responsibilities and my obligation to owe no one anything except to love one another (Rom.13.8). What greater human freedom is there in the kingdom of God than the freedom to love my neighbour as myself? When we fear the plea for economic reform we must examine whether our fear of social change and social justice is fuelled by our complacency and vested interests in unjust structures. We must ask whether we are seduced into undermining the health of the whole organism of the polis by contributing to the cancerous growth of individual cells over against the common weal. The hope which weans us from the religion of individualism is the gospel proclamation that love binds me to my brother and sister even as it binds me to God and 'perfect love casts out fear'.

According to Scripture, independent self-realization, like its close relation, self-justification, is an impossibility and an illusion. Why? Because to be human is to be made in God's image, is to be in relationship, as God himself is a relationship of love. To be human is to be made for a purpose beyond our self. Even the most gifted need other people, and need them all the more, if this was only understood. In fact, unless the strong develop the capacity both to give and to receive help from others they can never reach their true potential. Unless we acknowledge this, we become stuck playing the role of 'rugged individualist'. We will carry on this distortion of our humanity by denying our honest need for care and love, by denying our weaknesses and limits. This encourages pretence, dishonesty, and uses ridicule to reinforce the imbalanced emphasis. The biblical model for healthy and holy life envisions not individualism, but a community of inter-dependent persons, parts of a body, bearing one another's burdens as well as taking up and bearing one's own burdens, with the strong having a special obligation to honour the weaker members (Rom. 15.1). What is true for Church is true and just for the city as well, for the Lord of the Church is the Lord of all other lords. Whereas freedom for the individualist is a personal possession which is an inalienable right, freedom for the disciple in community flows out of communion with the truth. Recognizing and developing one's strengths through feedback, and exploring in a supportive environment one's weaknesses, and confessing one's sins in both areas, is the model for Christian community. The greater and lesser gifts are shared in a mutual love and the lesser is honoured all the more:

> On the contrary, the parts of the body which seem to be weaker are indispensable, and those parts of the body which we think less honourable we invest with the greater honour . . . But God has so adjusted the body, giving the greater honour to the inferior part, that there may be no discord in the body, but that the members may have the same care for one another . . . If one member suffers, all suffer together; if one member is honoured, all rejoice together. (1 Cor. 12.22–26)

The Seed Growing Secretly: Matthew 13.31–32.

When Jesus picked up a towel to wash the feet of the twelve, it was customary for a servant to perform that task. No one else rushed to do it. We know James and John preferred power. Peter's idea of authority did not include something as menial as foot-washing. Who knows what discomfort Judas felt. But Jesus has barely begun. The serving quality of love's authority descends further to bearing the burden of our sin on the cross. When God comes to redeem his creation, he does not cater to our pride. So to heal us he comes by the back entrance, as a lowly babe of a subjugated people, with questions of legitimacy surrounding his birth, a child not of the palace, but of the manger. One day he draws water, towel-in-hand to wash our feet, the next day he shall wash us with his own blood. His authority came among us as one who served.

The enormity of the change in the way people who name themselves Christians exercise authority and power percolates down slowly, but inexorably. As people baptized into Jesus Christ pondered, remembered, and experienced Jesus's authority, the crisis in the use of authority rippled out into their social history.

Consider the monarchy of Great Britain. Sir Charles Firth describes the culminating moment following the English Civil War, as even the stoutest supporters of Parliament's army, having defeated Charles I, gasp in awe as the king's head is lopped off and rolls. They are shocked at the enormity of what they have rejected. The ancient identity between monarchial bloodline and legitimate government as a divine right has been shattered.[5] Henceforth the monarchy's moral authority remains highest when its representatives are seen to be servants of the people. Its present and future value is most under threat when it seems to exist largely for its own self-indulgence and privilege.

Similarly, parliament's authority shall be legitimate to the extent it represents and serves the people. Only later does this result in increasingly democratic elections, but the long journey to this political translation turns an unrepeatable corner nevertheless. The root of this evolution springs from the biblical Hebraic tradition with its profound respect for the weak as well as the strong, the deliverance of the enslaved Hebrew people from Egypt, and the entry of the One who told stories of prodigals welcomed home, of one lost sheep so valued that it was searched for and found, and who himself led us by serving, the leader who washes the feet of his people. Each person is seen as an end, not a means, intrinsically valuable, with the rulers having the responsibility to protect and secure the well-being of the people. The seed for this transformation was planted when the disciples believed that God had revealed his sovereign majesty most pointedly by washing their feet. Democratic government firmly translates into politics love's affirmation that even lost sheep, even thieves on the cross, matter to the Messiah who came among us as one who served. A personal vote in a representational system enshrines the accountability of leaders to serve and the state exists to serve and to be accountable to the smallest, least powerful unit of the community, the individual. Balancing our respect for the individual is the reciprocal commitment of the person to the community. My purpose is simply nothing more nor less than to regard and love my neighbour, in the same way that I regard and love myself.

Many times within the kingdoms of earth justice seems a lost cause. When in 1982 Bishop Desmond Tutu received the Nobel Peace Prize for pursuing non-violent transformation of a racist South Africa, he was asked at the time if such a strategy was not naive in an essentially unjust society. Tutu replied that his hope was alive because ever since Jesus was killed and put in the ground on Good Friday, but then rose on the third day, he was a prisoner of hope. The future of South Africa is yet to be written, but the changes there have been astonishing despite the threat of violence, not because of it.

Each generation of the Church wrestles with the social implications of gospel love. But an economic translation is a recurrent ingredient. It started with Pentecost itself, when: 'All who believed were together and had all things in common, and they sold their possessions and goods and distributed them to all, each according to their need' (Acts 3.44). In the Middle Ages, monasteries and guilds were created by the Church to be islands of community and brotherhood in a sea of harsh and cruel tribalism and fiefdoms. These colonies eventually burst out of their walls and memberships to touch whole nations and societies with the vision that peoples are intrinsically not units of labour or property but collections of free persons equally loved and in need of grace. In the 18th century, Wesley's revival enormously impacted the social life of England, from Wilberforce's campaign against slavery to the founding of the trade union movement. The 19th century saw the rise of Kingsley and Maurice and the 'Christian socialism' which in anger and compassion challenged the exploitation of child labour, the sweat-shops and the predatory monopolies. The writings of Charles Dickens gave a dramatic focus and mass impetus to transform British society into a place where a stranger was a brother, and the nation would not be left ever again to the anarchy from above, in which the weak and unprotected were only pawns in a game played by others.

Let us remind ourselves: what after all is the chief sign that a community is a community of faith in Jesus Christ? Is it essentially masterly gifts of preaching or tongues or healing, cognitively captivating doctrines, beautiful rituals? According to the New Testament, it is none of these: 'By this shall all men know you are my disciples, if you have love one for another.' St Paul elaborates further in the classic discussion of church life in 1 Corinthians 13:

> If I speak in the tongues of men and of angels, but have not love, I am a noisy gong or a clanging cymbal. And if I have prophetic powers, and understand all mysteries and all knowledge, and if I have all faith, so as to remove mountains but have not love, I am nothing. If I give away all I have, and if I deliver my body to be burned, but have not love, I gain nothing. (1 Cor. 13.1–3)

Why does the New Testament so emphasize love as the defining feature of Christian community? Because God in his innermost being is an intimate community of love–Father, Son, and Holy Spirit. God is not occasionally or arbitrarily, but essentially, a communion of love. Therefore since the first days Christians declared that Jesus, not Caesar, is Lord (*kurios*) of lords and King of kings, the Church has insistently witnessed that the earthly polis cannot simply be ignored or set apart as an autonomous government with its own laws and order quite separated and unrelated to the law of love and the Lordship of Christ. Because Jesus was not a private, household god, who kept out of public life, but the Lord of heaven and earth, the early Church refused to declare Caesar as Lord, even on pain of persecution and martyrdom. A love of God with no mission to teach society the ways of love, reduces Christianity to a private religious club, and reduces Jesus to a personal talisman, a household god who exists for the sake of our personal salvation. Instead, disciples bear witness to a new community where each is precious and valued, and which prophesies that the loving reign of God has come to redeem all things, through the unique power of Jesus Christ, crucified and risen. God is never only *my* Father in heaven, he is *our* Father.

Mission as Coming Home: The Method is the Message

Our mission to transform the world according to the ways of love is either secured or undercut by the manner and methods through which it is pursued. Often the Church's mission has been described using military metaphors, the church militant, the mighty army of Christian soldiers marching as to war with our evangelistic crusades and rallies. Surely St Paul had a profound reason for describing a Christian as a spiritual warrior armed with the whole armour of God. But it is important that we design our battle strategy according to the way of the warrior depicted by the 'Dream of the Rood', who laid aside his armour and mounted the cross. The final description of our mission is that of a home-coming, a journey towards home where the Father spreads a banquet for prodigals. To paraphrase Chesterton, going to church is like going to God's pub, for there we go to be filled with the Holy Spirit, until that day when we shall reach the ultimate inn at the end of our journey where we shall drink from the flagons of the Father's love for the Son and the Son's for the Father.[6] What one does at an inn is not essentially to conduct committee meetings or plan battles. The chief end of Church and of our mission, is to enjoy God, and the love of God is better than wine. The army of God is a most peculiar kind, with the most unique manner of weaponry, whose weapons are utterly unorthodox according to the standards of earthly warfare. The peace which results is not like the notions of peace we learn elsewhere. In this journey towards peace our sorrow and joy are gathered up into our home which is Father, Son and Spirit.

What are we fighting for? Perhaps the dominant tragedy of Christian mission activity is our neglect of home in preference for a flurry of activism. It reflects itself in our neglect of enjoying God in worship and prayer. It reflects itself in group propensities to become diverted into the various goal-avoiding behaviours we have already discussed. It reflects itself in our tendency to over-invest in programmes and careers, and to leave our home relationships to take care of themselves. And they do not. We fail to plan or schedule time to play and pray and worship and, not surprisingly, we become over-extended and undernourished. We burn out.

Christians should ponder the tragic story of the committed communists Ruth First and Joe Slovo, who were totally dedicated to the moral mission of changing South Africa. But as an adult, in her book and the film, *World's Apart*, their daughter describes their missionary zeal from the point of view of a child growing up in this totally dedicated home. There was no time for home or family. She received left-overs and boarding-school. She was alienated, estranged, and resentful of their mission. This tragic story could be written about many committed church leaders' families. The most important sign of the Christian movement, that which the world most needs to see, is not an army, but the taste of home. When we visit the sick or the prisoner, and feed the hungry, this essentially is what we offer them. We offer them home. When the Father ran down the streets of his village to embrace the prodigal, it was a welcome home. Our homes, villages, cities, and nations all need the healing welcome of home.

Meanwhile, we are homesick in our homes, torn by quarrels, rivalries, neglect or spoiling. Our homes and our cities need a greater home. That is why Christ, the homeless one, died for our homes. The experience of love and being loved needs to be felt in our homes, our places of work, our cities, and towns. To isolate these from one another, as if family is what happens in houses but not in cities or offices or factories, is to make a distinction that salves our avoidant consciences. Members of the human family toil in every city or province where institutions and corporate structures cry out to be interpreted through the lenses of Christian mission to call people home. Christian mission in the polis and the Church is home dashing down the streets to embrace us in love. Our worship and our work merely reflect the sprint of the Father to the Son. Jesus is after all, Immanuel, God with us, companion, advocate. Though we face pain and death, he is home's surprising coming to us. Our being embraced is our coming home.

Our map of the journey home to love, or love's journey to bring us home, has extended outward all the way from the self to the social and political sphere. There is another way to map our journey into love. This way divides the journey into three parts: the beginning (the origins of love); the way (of suffering); and the triumphant ending (the conquest of evil). To this itinerary we now turn.

Notes

1   Richard Armstrong, *Hawaii*, (Hampton, Virginia: Normal School Press, 1887), p. 64.

2   Augustine, *City of God*, (Image Books, 1958) (AD 426), pp. 15–16.

3   Charles E. B. Cranfield, 'The Christian's Political Responsibility

According to the New Testament', (*SJT* 15, 1962), *The Bible and Christian Life*, (T & T Clark), p. 53.

4   *City of God*, pp. 87–88.

5   Sir Charles Firth, *Oliver Cromwell and the Rule of the Puritans in England*, (Oxford University Press, [1857], 1966), p. 225.

6   G. K. Chesterton, *Charles Dickens, The Last of the Great Men*, (Readers Club, [1906], 1942), p. 212.

PART TWO

7

The Origins of Love and Hate

An Ancient Controversy

We have mapped a journey into love that has looked at our experience of what love is, what it is not, and how self, marriage, family, church, and community experience love's purposes. There is another way to chart the terrain of love's landscape and this is to consider love's origin, its developmental process, and its final destiny. That is, how did love originate, what path must it take to grow, and given the immensity of the obstacles, what is the hope of its triumph?

Cultures ancient and modern have offered stories or myths which interpret both love's importance to the community and its relation to love's great adversary, hatred. Inevitably, the origins of love and hate are closely related to the ancient question of the relation between good and evil. There are two well-known stories from the ancient world about the origin of good and evil which rehearse this recurrent theme as the conflict between light and darkness, order and chaos, and good and evil.

Around 2,000 BC the Babylonians told the story of the male god Apsu and the female deity Tiamat, who begot a thousand gods to populate heaven. Then one day (perhaps in an interesting projection into the heavens of Babylonian family life), the children quarrel with the male god, Apsu, and he is slain. Thereafter, war breaks out between the widow of Apsu, Mother Tiamat, and her rebellious children. Old Mother Tiamat is an intimidating Shelob of chaotic darkness, modelled after or epitomized by the ambivalent life of the coastal villages off the sea. When the waters are tranquil, they provide food, transport, and employment for the village. But when volatile like a tidal wave, the swirling water devours her children. The little gods barely stand a chance against her. Who can stand against such a dreaded mother of all monsters? Finally, arises their son, Marduk (who happens to be

the city god of Babylon), the god of light and creativity. He alone
manages to defeat his mother and from her dead, but fertile,
carcass, he fashions creation. Thus arises humankind, made from
the blood of the dead goddess, Tiamat. Each year the people
dramatically re-enact this struggle between order and chaos, light
and darkness, fertility and decay. Epitomized by the growing
season, and the nurturing but threatening ambivalence of chaotic
mother nature, neither side reigns supreme. Babylon worships
Marduk and hopes for protection, but chaos re-emerges to
threaten the people with destruction. So it is that light and
darkness, and love and hate, perpetually quarrel. Human hopes
dangle between these two equal and opposite forces. Marduk,
representing order and society, ever lies in danger of being
swallowed up again by the hostile sea of Mother Tiamat.

Another ancient epic of the Mediterranean world, the story of
Gilgamesh, describes the spirit of this struggle. Gilgamesh is the
hero who searches for, and finds, the plant of life. Tragically,
by carelessness, he loses it. Just as Gilgamesh is nearly overwhelmed by grief, a goddess comes and consoles him, recalling
to his mind that life is for the gods and death is for humans.
The rather hedonistic moral the comforting goddess brings is
not lost to ancients or moderns: life, order, and light has its
time; then there is chaos, darkness and death. Hopeless and
inevitable is the struggle between the two. Therefore enjoy life
and its pleasures until death comes.

The Hebraic Alternative

Having recalled these ancient stories, both illustrating an overwhelming dualism between good and evil, let us hear the familiar
Hebrew story with new ears. The Mesopotamian myths were well
known. Listeners no doubt expect to hear another variant on this
perpetual conflict:

> And God said, 'Let there be light'; and there was light. And
> God saw that the light was good; and God separated the
> light from the darkness. God called the light Day, and the
> darkness he called Night. And there was evening and there
> was morning, one day. (Gen. 1.3–5)

On it goes through to day seven's sabbatical celebration.
What happened to the mighty conflict between good and evil,

light and darkness, order and chaos? Simply stated, good and evil are not the dual faces of ultimate reality battling endlessly for supremacy. The good Lord simply speaks order. He makes good things. Unlike deities locked in immortal combat, Genesis presents us with a creative, co-operative plurality of One ('let us') working as calmly and peacefully as a carpenter in his shop. Not primary and equal with goodness and light, evil and chaos do not enter until the third chapter and only then as intruders with little or no explanation of their origin.

The good Lord of the Hebrew people has no rivals and no equal. His eternal domain is not an eternal stalemate, like that of Marduk or Gilgamesh. His government is gracious. His power and authority are discharged with the air of giving permission ('Let there be . . .'), not giving orders to dominate chaos. His authority expresses itself by investing worth and justice into creation; he is not a cosmic social Darwinist who expects creation to lift itself up by its own boot-straps and prove its worth. Not proven, not earned, creation's value is sheer gift. Inevitably this means that in the Hebrew vision, the very structure of a beloved creation has joy built into it. The rivers clap their hands, the mountains shout and sing for joy (Ps. 98.8). Why? Because in the presence of the Lord is a beloved and peaceful order which is not at war with itself. Whereas struggling to earn value, win praise, and compete for worth creates anxiety and limits our creativity, receiving our value as an endowment creates joy and a spontaneous echo of the Creator's creativity in reciprocating exploration and play. Creation is such a place because it has been made by the good Lord in whom there is no darkness.

Seen in this way, the Hebrew story could not stand in greater contrast from the others. In the ancient dualism, love and hate, and order and chaos are gripped in co-eternal combat. In the Hebrew story, love reigns supreme and creates in freedom. Remember, evil has no place in the story until chapter three. When Jesus retells the creation story in his parable recorded in Matthew 13.24–30, he reinforces this emphasis. There he portrays evil as sneaking into the garden to sow weeds by night, under cover of darkness. Evil is hardly co-equal with the plan and power of the farmer. Despite the intruder, the farmer shall not abandon his good intentions nor destroy his crop: 'Let both grow together until the harvest.'

Modern Myths of Love's Origins

Modern healers of the human psyche, seeking to analyse the
conflicting emotions of their contemporaries, strikingly resemble
the alternative visions of the ancient Mesopotamians and the
Hebraic vision of Genesis. Despite their many differences, consider the commitment of Sigmund Freud and Melanie Klein to
the theory of the death instinct. It alleges that we have an innate
drive for destruction and evil which is the equal of our creative
urge to love and life (cf., Tiamat and Marduk). If as a pastor or
care-giver, I am trained in these assumptions, when you come to
me for help I shall regard you, not by assuming your worth and
desire for wholeness and love, but with the reservations, scepti-
cism and mixed feelings appropriate to the intrinsic and eternal
mixture which you are. My therapeutic goal is to build your ego
strength by controlling your amoral pleasure tendencies (id), and
easing your ego's tension as it lives between the harsh demand
of your conscience (superego) and your drive for pleasure.
Remember, you are as essentially evil as you are essentially good.
One is not prior to the other. When I look at you thus, I no doubt
anticipate you will react to my ambivalent regard by responding
according to your previous experiences of conditional love.

But what if creation is not inherently dualist, but instead 'a
good thing spoiled'? Even John Calvin, who reflected more
systematically on the doctrine of the fall than most theologians,
did not conceive of the divine image as being obliterated, but
understood that an 'awareness of divinity' remains inscribed
on every heart.[1] However, because our sense of God's presence
is corrupted, it produces the bad fruit of superstition instead of
faith, idolatry instead of adoration and hatred instead of love.
Our disfigured awareness of God leads into an intensifying spiral
of error. The Christian doctrine of the total depravity of humankind does not mean everything is essentially evil or as corrupt
as it could be. Nor does it imply the creature can unilaterally
abolish his relation to, and identity as, a covenant partner with
his Creator. But our depravity does mean that everything is
tainted. All our faculties, even our prized capacities for knowledge and for love, need healing.

What happens when we look at each other with the lenses of
Genesis, as made in God's image, in whom there is no darkness?
What if we are essentially made for love and love is what satis-
fies, not de-tensioning the conflict between id and superego?

What if the goal of life is not social control but setting our passions free to enjoy their true purposes? Seen in this way, gratitude and envy, love and hate, are not co-essential attributes of our humanity. The latter in each pair are frustrated distortions of the former.

There are many related questions: What are the optimal conditions for human growth in love and maturity? How shall I regard my neighbours if I desire their growth and maturity in love? Shall I treat them with a dualistic ambivalence? Shall I make my regard for them conditional upon their acceptance of certain therapeutic theories and techniques? When I provide support and give counsel to someone, shall I regard them with suspicion and see my encounter with them as a dual of wits, or as a brother or sister whom God has made in his image for love and for good? What if they too, in their heart of hearts, despite their defences, confusions, fears, and angers, are searching for this goal for which they were created ?

When my children are angry or envious, shall I advise them to face and admit they are simply in touch with the angry, jealous, hateful part of themselves which is sheer naughtiness? In effect, shall I name them as evil? For example, 'You are just being lazy,' or, 'That is your envy coming out.' Or shall I pose myself and them a further question, namely, *why* are my children angry, or envious? What is missing? They were intended for and created in love. What has become twisted and discouraged? How can it be untwisted and courage restored? These are the questions which the Genesis story arouses me to ask. As Lewis has reminded us, God made all the pleasures. All the snake can do is twist and corrupt them. Our pleasures, emotions, and desires are fundamentally good because creation is good. So when I am angry and envious, do I call myself a sinner and leave it at that, or do I ask why this sinner has settled for a distortion which expresses itself in rage or jealousy? It makes all the difference whether I regard my child as a hater, who is essentially and irrationally prone to self-destruction, or whether I see hatred and jealousy as a complaint and cry for help because the deepest law of their being is being blocked and unfulfilled, and the anger, the envy or the refusal to pay attention is a result. This petulance, these lies, these avoidances, are not their ultimate identities. Hatred or envy points to a lack of something more basic, more ultimate which is absent, namely, love. Certainly once a person has endured systematic mistreatment, with defences conditioned to assume abandonment or impingement, it makes them nearly blind to genuine love and acceptance. Nevertheless how we look at people, and how we look at ourselves, makes a difference in how we treat the best and the worst, and in what kind of care we offer. How God looks at his creation matters even more.

These are the kind of questions which, in his own way, Ronald Fairbairn insisted on asking of Melanie Klein's psychological version of Tiamat and Marduk. Separated by his relative isolation in Edinburgh from the Freudian stronghold in London, Fairbairn pondered and developed further Klein's theory of interior psychic 'object-relations' which so influence and interpret our outer experiences of love and life, passing on the parents we have internalized from childhood and making them permanent aspects of our psyche. What if, queried Fairbairn, the reason we pursue pleasure in inappropriate and harmful ways is not the result of a blind, chaotic drive, but is born of frustration and discouragement? What if hatred and envy arise not simply because we innately identify with the bad inner parent, but because good psychic objects, that is, good and loving relationships, are unavailable and so we settle for temporary relief? Using psychological language, what if the libido is fundamentally object-seeking, that is, seeking a good relationship, not pleasure-seeking?[2] Fairbairn's psychological questions and the answers to which they pointed parallel the way C. S. Lewis came to interpret his search for joy. What he really longed for was not an experience of ecstasy or pleasure. These were but by-products of the attachment to a good and loving reality. Thus the goal in therapy now takes on two tasks: to interpret 'acting out' behaviours as discouraged substitutes for caring relationships; and to provide in therapy a loving, non-exploitative, non-abandoning relationship which over time creates good enough internal objects so that good relationships can develop outside the therapeutic environment.

Implications for a Theology of Redemption

When we turn to theology, shall we interpret 'original sin' to be the equal of original goodness or the description 'sinner' as a closed definition? I believe we are better advised to see our fellow 'sinner' in terms of an open-ended description which implies a frustrated, wounded sojourner whose very being as sinner is hounded by and cries out for redemption. Our very sinfulness witnesses to our need for healing by the sovereign Lord who created in love and called it all good. Alongside creation, 'original sin' is not quite so original as it may sound. It is an intruder. Within the context of creation and redemption, to be 'sinners' can only be regarded as an incomplete and distorted experience. To build an entire theology and world view with sinfulness as our starting point is structurally akin to building an entire psychological theory around the basic assumptions of neurosis, pleasure-seeking libido, and the death instinct. It results in the experience of a highly ambivalent God. The ground is thus laid for religious people to fall into pride's twin errors: the self-justified pharisee, inflated with superiority at his self-assessment; or the self-condemned sinner, deflated with inferiority at his self-assessment and devoid of any assurance of God's love. Certainly church history is well acquainted with emphases which allege that God hardly loves his entire creation, but, for example, only that limited association of individuals who happen to subscribe to a prescribed list of doctrines, thus testifying to God's special preference of them over against others.

To ask how does God restore his disordered world is to focus on the person and work of Jesus Christ, the express image of God come among us. When Jesus Christ turns towards us, how does he see us? When the Holy Spirit broods upon our world, does he approach us with reserve or ambivalence? According to Jesus's parable about the sower, he sees the tares, the evil as parasitic intruder, not as the Father's intention for us. When the prodigal son is returning home, does the Father see an evil failure slinking home or a dearly loved son found at last? The disease of evil and hate is not an essential quality of the Father's creation. Christ neither condemns nor tries to shore up a weak ego in order to balance our destructive urges. He reaches out to restore these disfigurements to their proper purposes by the power of love.

As any physician knows, essential to the task of healing is the task of diagnosis. Unless my disease is named and confronted, it cannot be treated. For love's sake, the Spirit of Christ reveals to us our distortions, defences, and false interpretations (John 16.8). But our re-creation is based on the claim that we were created for love's sake and that love is the essential song of our soul. Grace recreates what has become destructive, but which was intended for joy and love. The good Lord cannot create in neutrality or in tension, but only in the freedom of love. According to Genesis, this is the only way God creates. And the hope Christians have for all who experience the brokenness of sin is that the powers of chaos and darkness shall not have the last word, even as they did not share in the first word. Christian faith declares that Jesus Christ is more than a match for evil. And though he is the conqueror of sin, he is the good Shepherd of sinners. In the language of the nineteenth-century German pastors, father and son Blumhardt, the Father's charge to the Son was not to judge the world, or condemn it or have mixed feelings about it:

> Love my beloved world, no matter what you may experience, even if you are crucified, forgive them, for they do not know what they are doing. Love my world. I created it for love. I am the Father of all that lives in it and this Fatherhood I will not surrender. Every living creature is mine. They sprang from love and grace. Go, love the world. How it came to be in great darkness is a mystery, but there is no darkness in me. You are the Son of my light and love, the Son of the Father who loves the world.[3]

Conditionality: How our Personal Experience of Fallenness Arises

If God who is good, created us in love and for love, how did we come to be spoiled, come to hate? The story of the fall occurs in chapter three of Genesis. When believers ask the question of the origins of that which is not equal with God, but a misuse of good gifts, we gaze beyond the boundaries of light and order into the darkness. What we are able to see is limited. For instance, we are not told where or how the serpent comes to be there. Like the intruder in Jesus's parable, he sneaks in. Nor is there any explanation why Adam and Eve should be tempted to mistrust God due to some inadequacy of God's provision. Nonetheless when evil slinks in, it leads to a lack, a privation, an emptiness. Here it expresses a lack of confidence or faith in God's faithfulness and provision. Why this should arise also lacks any positive explanation. There is no Tiamat or any other malignant causal material. But though we are faithless, the good Lord remains faithful. Even the expulsion from the garden contains God's protection and promise of deliverance.

To a greater or lesser degree, we have all grown up with this experience of lack of love, or the impinging presence of non-love. The result of this devaluation imprints upon us a corresponding identity of being deprived. We experience ourselves as depraved, unwelcome, and fallen. When our beloved gazes upon us, we see shame in their eyes, not the glad pleasure in our presence we had anticipated. We now feel ashamed of ourselves. Perhaps the defining feature of this shaming or disinvestment experience is conditionality. John Powell describes how early on we receive the subtle message, if you are good, if you do not cry, if you eat your dinner, if you act like a big boy, if you earn good marks . . . people shall be very proud of you, they shall love you. But because love is in short supply, unless you negotiate all these 'ifs', you may be left out in the cold. Consequently when we missed the mark, when we woke crying in the middle of the night, made a mess of our food and so on, we absorbed our parents' irritation and rejection. As parents, we rely on levers which we instinctively know how to push and pull at the right moment to create the desired result: smiles and frowns, warmth and coldness, words and silence. Thus, love becomes something we lack and something we must earn as a reward for achievement. The sting in the tail is the threat that if you don't, no love shall be granted. Eric Fromm writes: 'To be loved because of one's merits because one deserves it, always leaves doubt. . . . There is always a fear that love could disappear . . . "deserved" love easily leaves a bitter feeling one is not loved for oneself, but is loved only because one pleases, that one is, in the last analysis, not loved at all but used.'[4]

Conditionality is the inner message which most thoroughly promotes the distorted idea that worth and love must be earned or self-generated. Gone is the Creator's gracious decision to lovingly invest us with worth: 'It is good.' In this chaotic, anxious experience of having to purchase love we may sell anything, even our soul. Now emerges the competitive struggle between pride's anxious inflation and its discouraged deflation. What are the results? My work and my play cease to mirror the harmony of the Creator's creativity, and reveal instead an envious struggle with my neighbour for limited and conditional quantities of love and even the necessities of life. My tasks shall not be done, like Abel, gladly for the pleasure of doing that which is intrinsically valuable work; but like Cain, I toil in order to prove myself, win power, and garner approval. The scent of self-justification and desperation spoils my offering. I become caught in the spiral of working for my advantage and inevitably for the disadvantage of my neighbour. Predatory relationships replace mutuality. A family of interdependence, with members' differing gifts mutually valued is replaced by the apparent independence of the strong and the dependence of the weak. The more I experience love as conditional, the more it creates in me the feeling that I am not lovable except when I am dominant by asserting my worth over another or when I am the centre of attention. This frustration and disappointment in love's absence or non-love's domination leads to the experience of anger. In other words, anger and its aftermath of hate are not irreducible character traits. They are signs of the absence of love. They are closely related to privation and the sense of something good which has been taken away. From this inner disfigurement emerge the political and social structures which mirror and re-enforce our wounded identities.

The Birth of Anger

Hatred arises when anger's frustrations in love are not permitted expression but are driven underground. An abscess of resentment becomes the shadow atmosphere erupting into and poisoning further relationships. It is easy for moralizers to spot the sin of the angry, disobedient child. It is closer to the truth, and more painful for adult moralizers, to see the naughtiness as part of a relational network. Depending on the severity of the conditions extracted from the child before love is supplied, the distorted love network spawns frustration, rage, or even hopelessness. To label someone as bad, envious, or naughty without exploring the causes of the frustration, is an invitation to the severing of a relationship. We can only surmise that to receive such a parenting strategy from infancy and then to have it enshrined in psychological theory, as was the case for Melanie Klein's own daughter, makes her refusal to attend her mother's funeral, though she lived in the same city, not only understandable but inevitable. Pedagogy which encourages us to 'break the child's will' easily seduces us into relating to our children very much in a dominance-submission model with inevitable consequences of revolt and rebellion. Much depends on the extent to which a parent's own experience of love has been a Genesis gift or an ambivalent Babylonian reward.

A minister was busily engaged in painting and redecorating the church. It had become a magnificent obsession. Meanwhile, with mother away for a fortnight, younger daughter in a display of sheer naughtiness (or was it simply an indirect way to communicate her anger?), daubed a brushful of white paint on the varnished wooden door. The minister exploded internally with holy indignation. Fortunately, he was surrounded by a great cloud of witnesses, his fellow painters, so his daughter received a very controlled rebuke. More fortunately, he was able to do something his daughter had not yet received permission to do safely, that is, share his own hurt and anger with a wiser and older colleague, without being made to feel ashamed. The colleague said: 'Sounds like she's really angry at you.' The more he thought about it, the more the church struck him as the perfect indirect target. Indeed, daddy seemed to be spending all his time on this old building and mummy was absent. How could she fail to be jealous of such competition? Later that week she firmly disobeyed a simple request to start getting ready for a bath and bed. Instead of naming her as a naughty child, he stopped, looked with calm acceptance into her eyes and said: 'You're really angry with me, aren't you?' Her fierce face visibly relaxed into calm. Just to be understood, to have her frustration acknowledged, was the beginning of a sea change in their relationship. One young child's indirect expression of anger through disobedience had been interrupted on its journey to becoming hatred. Without further protest, the child had the bath. Somehow the embrace of being understood made this parental request no longer a burdensome provocation.

Indirection and Scapegoating

We often aim our anger at indirect targets such as churches in order to protect a source too dangerous to hate for fear of losing it. In the case of a young child, that which she needs most is her parents. Hence the rebellion of anger takes the form of defacing something highly valued by the parent, for example, the church, school-work, or something a parent insists upon. If dad continues to lavish attention on his job and be miserly in his time with the child, and if she is not allowed to identify or have her frustration acknowledged, for such an attitude is taboo, her rebellion will likely increase. Very rarely do children permit themselves the luxury of hating their parents. This would make us orphans. Safer targets may include the obvious rivals for parental love, namely, brothers and sisters or the job which takes them away from us. In a remarriage, the new partner is a splendid target to launch anger towards. Of course as teenage years draw on, increased independence becomes increasingly attractive. A little angry display of independence to test the limits is rather a stimulating exercise. But for many of us, some of the time at least, parents can be quite nice. Despite our protests, we remain dependent in many ways. So who does one daub with paint?

Hatred is difficult to root out because it so conveniently attaches itself to indirect targets–Jews, Arabs, Protestants, Roman Catholics, for example–depending on your culturally permissible targets. Racism is an externalized, safe expression of hatred. The true source of anger which grows into hate usually remains hidden because it would be too dangerous or too humiliating to face the source. We lay our blame and rage on another in order to let some of the livid lava escape before we internally explode. The children in the playground bully the boy who is too thin, too heavy, too tall, too short, too clever, too slow, too light, too dark. Hating the one who is different, we project and scapegoat the weakness, inferiority, or limitations we have learned to despise in ourselves and in our families. We cannot risk admitting or exploring the origins of such self-destructive hate. So we project the inner crisis outside and attack external enemies. The log in my own eye is projected and seen in my brothers' (Matt. 7.3).

If an honest confession of anger or disappointment is shamed as taboo, it hides underground and forms an abscess of negative emotion. It is only as we are given permission to allow our anger to be exposed without humiliation or condemnation, that it can be drained of its pain. If we do not face our anger, we project it elsewhere, daubing paint onto other targets. Sometimes when there are no other safe targets, we take the hate out on ourselves.

Self-Hate

Peter had spent half of his life disliking himself. He was raised in a household where his committed parents with born-again zeal pointed out the rules of their church without reference to the necessary preamble of love and grace. By adolescence his faults and failures had been picked apart with a fine tooth comb. He was never permitted to 'talk back'. If he began to express anger he was banished to his room because a good Christian boy ought not to be angry especially after all his devout parents have done for him. Nonetheless he found himself acting out his unexpressed rage toward various outer authority figures he would encounter: school authorities; police and their petty rules about small-time theft or arson. The list of misconduct was endless. Relationships with peers were similarly dissatisfying, either superficial or severed by mistrust. Only in his twenties did he discover the root of his confusion when he was able to explore with a wise therapist that he had swallowed not a little rage at his parents and perhaps at God for sanctioning such a 'godly' domicile or 'prison'. Since the anger had stayed hidden so long because it was so unacceptable, it had become hatred. This was a very painful realization. At least he now knew why he had such self-hate as well. It was the final refuge in protecting himself from facing the darker truth about his feelings towards his 'good Christian' parents and the god who was on their side. It was easier to hate and blame himself for all his inadequacies and badness out of loyalty to his family than to face his own anger towards his parents. At least, if he himself was the 'baddie', he might change. If parents and their powerful gods are the 'baddies', our situation is grim indeed.

And the final object of rage of course is God. The emotional soil for atheism lies here. We may be frustrated or furious at the hand he has dealt us. Yet it seems a rather dangerous thing to be angry with the omnipotent source. It makes sense to vent our anger at something or someone who may represent the source, but has a bit less fire-power with which to respond, and is more credibly guilty of incompetence; a parent, a priest, or a teacher often provides a safer target to shoot at than God. But when these are misdirected targets, we make war on the very ones who might provide support.

Good Grief: The Transition from Hatred

When my anger is finally faced and identified in a gracious environment, it has no further reason to exist and may gradually or
even rapidly diminish. Soon, however, another strong feeling
takes its place: sadness. Perhaps this doesn't seem to herald better
days but there is a time to mourn, to grieve the lack of tenderness or guidance from the parents or friends to whom one has
been so close but from whom one feels so far away. Along with
our grief over what we have not experienced, we also are finally
free to feel sadness over what in rebellion we have become: a
brooding legion of resentments, fears, compensating greeds, lusts,
and shallow cruelties; an inability to be genuine, for fear our real
feelings are not acceptable, an inability to listen, to care, so self-
absorbed have we become in our inner world of unmet need.
Unless this transition that is grieving occurs, we are doomed to
cut off our feelings altogether and live exclusively out of our
intellect or problem-solving gear; pursue religion or work in a
way which has little space for emotion. We will prefer reading
papers filled with facts to dialogue with our children, our
partner, or anyone else with whom we live in close quarters. We
will prefer common-room banter or 'happy hour' diversions to
intimacy. We will prefer the analysis of doctrines, with generous
amounts of time arguing over their meaning or relevance, to an
open dialogue of the heart with the One Jesus invites us to call
'Abba', or Daddy.

Good Anger

What enables the transition from rage to grief and repentance
to occur? Surely not being scolded for our narcissistic self-
absorption. It is rather the experience that our hurt and our
anger are not a disgrace but the witness in our own souls to the
sorrow of God. Our anguished 'no' to injustice is not against God
as if we are rebels against a divinely sanctioned status quo, but
the prophetic groan of the Spirit sighing and longing within
our spirits, testifying that He is alongside us, knowing the pain
as his own and bearing it with us and through us. God's own
angry 'no' against all evil is but glimpsed when Jesus warns
those who cause little ones to stumble (Matt. 18.6). Knowing
his advocacy in the depths of our darkness, that we are freely
accepted, not condemned as we anticipated, permits us access

to a new quality of intimacy. For the One whose sheer goodness creates and recreates has no loyalty to cruel laws and unjust order. His righteousness entails his own tragic intervention and identification with all who have been afflicted and persecuted.

What analogy will this experience of God's advocacy have in our parenting? If we are not to provoke our children to wrath (Eph. 6.4), we must learn how to give children permission to communicate their sorrows and angers. I do not mean that we offer them a licence to rage and roar as future tyrants in training. But we can speak about our frustrations and discuss anger instead of either shouting about it or forbidding it by enforcing a rule that we swallow it in shame. A child's disobedience need no longer be labelled 'naughty' and driven underground. Disobedience may be due to many factors besides anger, including fatigue or hunger, which good listening may diagnose. Let us together explore our angers and the disappointments which give rise to misplaced aggression and disobedience. As we examine our own strong, angry reaction to behaviours we dislike, we may discover its roots in the ways our own frustration and anger were (dis)regarded by others. This can revolutionize both parent and child behaviour, not simply having the strong dictate to the weak, or allowing the weak to use the 'weak' reactions of shouting or crying to subtly dominate family conflicts. This way shall lead both parents and children into significant change. Father may find more space for domestic work and play in a life over-balanced by work schedule, pressure, and the need to be successful. Daughters and sons may discover they do not need to be naughty or provocative to receive personal attention. They may discover that work and play need not be polar opposites, but are mutually necessary components in family and at school.

Again, what frees us to flush out the poisons of unresolved anger is the same discovery that Job and Jeremiah, and many others, made throughout the pages of Scripture. God does not condemn our anger. God himself has anger, or wrath, as a crucial component of his love. Consider how the light of the Holy Spirit shines upon our hearts. This light penetrates to the joints and marrows, into the dark places we are ashamed of and therefore hide for fear they are unacceptable. This light penetrates in order to disclose and to interpret the privations and depravities from which our disobedience multiplies. Within the furnace of love's holy fire we discover more about ourselves than we wanted to know for fear of being burnt up. But the fire of God's anger against sin does not burn in order to incinerate us, but to purify and refine, cleansing and re-forging a precious new creation. To discover that our God is a consuming fire (Heb.12.29) is also to discover that self-righteous condemnation only pours fuel on the flames of our own hurt and rage, whereas the fire of holy love purifies our anger. The Holy Spirit of love interprets to us the meaning of our anger, convicts us of our impurities, and reveals our darkness always and unconditionally in the service of being our advocate. That is why wherever the Spirit of the Lord is, there is liberty. This light exposes not to condemn but to heal.

In other words, the Spirit sifts out our destructive rebellion from our constructive protest. He speaks his 'no' of judgement to our self-destructive 'acting out' behaviour in order to restore the hurting, wounded child of God who has learned to defend himself by hiding his hurt in aloof retreat or the bravado of aggression. These are the hidden wounds which the light exposes and interprets. The surprise is that he penetrates the darkness, not to reject but to restore us. In Jesus, we discover that the lion of Judah is also the lamb who comes to interpret, to bear, and to forgive our anger and sorrow. He takes these into himself on the cross. There he makes with us communion at those very distorted places where we, the agents both of aggressive crucifixion and weak compliance, in shame had expected only further rejection and further punishment: 'This then is how we know that we belong to the truth, and how we set our hearts at rest in his presence whenever our hearts condemn us. For God is greater than our hearts, and he knows everything' (1 John 3.19, 20). As a result, we enjoy the freedom to gladly repent because the light enters our darkness for love's sake, in an 'at-one-ment' of love no human parent or companion can ever provide.

The Secret Hidden Behind our Hate

Many in our culture have no trouble expressing their anger, though as we have seen, it is too often directed indirectly, its meaning is lost, and we are locked into compulsive repetition of angry or violent behaviours. But whether by misdirected expression or repression, there is a final reason we hide from facing the true sources of our anger even to ourselves, for as long as possible. If I express my anger at my parents, I run the danger of being overwhelmed by their anger at me. If I dare tell God I am angry with how things are working out in my life, I risk divine rejection and hell itself. What hides behind our hate? Fear. The threat of punishment and the greatest punishment of all, abandonment, often blocks our acknowledgement of hate.

I avoid facing the wound behind my anger not only because I sense that simply expressing anger is potentially destructive. It is a show of bravado to cover my fear. I may use anger as a means to power, to make the other party submit or at least avoid submission myself. But the desire for power through aggression and dominance is a discouraged substitute for love. Multiple displays of anger not only fail to cast out fear, they reinforce a chaotic reign of terror within. They further intensify and fortify our barricade against naming our fear.

To trust someone with feelings of anger is only sensible and hopeful if I dare believe I am unconditionally loved and that even my anger has worth and meaning. Only then do I feel free to face my anger and the losses which provoke it, and struggle through until there is no more reason to hate. It takes courage, not to act out, but to admit our rage. It takes confidence in love. Fear hides the problem for fear that if we reveal it, we shall be rejected. But concealing our fears leaves us full of pent-up emotion, guilt and anxiety. The other side of stoutly denying the problem is the depression resulting from the mental exhaustion of keeping the lid on all our negative feelings for fear of their consequences. Others may disguise their fears by channelling their energy into a plethora of activities, keeping so busy they do not have time to stop and think.

Fear settles for pseudo-relationships, with God and with everyone else. We see this in the stock answers fed to Job by his comforters: 'Bad things happen to bad people', 'You must be hiding some sin', 'You must be guilty or this would not have happened'. Their fear-based logic also reasons that God will not love us if we tell him we are angry or frustrated or disappointed. But God contradicts the logic of fear when he receives Job's complaints and anger. As a result, Job discovers intimacy with God, leaving behind the platitudes of his pious contemporaries.

In Georges Bernanos' novel, *The Diary of a Country Priest*, the young priest's childlike candour disarms a staunch lady of the parish into facing the frightening truth that her indifference and resignation towards God hides the fact that she hates her husband for his numerous affairs, her daughter for the attention she gives her husband, and God for allowing her favourite child to die in infancy. In fact her entire life has been a life consumed with the hidden flames of hate and jealousy hidden behind the general bossiness by which she dominates the household. She rears like a viper: 'I've ceased to bother about God. When you've forced me to admit that I hate him, will you be any better off, you idiot?' The priest replies: 'You no longer hate him. Hate is indifference and contempt. Now at last you're face to face with him!'[5] She is stunned by the priest into facing the fact that her contempt hides both her hatred and her fear that God has abandoned her and shall continue to do so. The priest further shocks her by not condemning her, but in an unforgettable way grieving with her over the loss of her beloved son. Only now after many years is she free to cry out and exorcise her rage. Only now can she feel alive again after blocking off her vitality with the suppressed rage of indifference and the need to dominate the household. Just hours before she dies, she writes a letter to the priest thanking him for now at last she is at peace.

The Beginning of Wisdom?

As believers continue to testify, the gospel of God's love in Christ not only turns the old world but also old words upside-down, baptizing them into the way of Jesus. For example, if love is the purpose behind the Creator's design, somewhere in the back of our minds we may be wondering how to reconcile the conclusion that perfect love casts out fear (1 John 4.18) with the Old Testament dictum that the fear of the Lord is the beginning of wisdom (Prov. 1.7). Too often this wisdom saying has been interpreted within a framework of dominance and submission, with the instinctive fear of powers greater than us overwhelming us. We fear those powers and seek to appease them by paying homage. When we worship a god of dominating power, not sacrificial love, faith is not so much a confidence in love, and a permission to explore, create, and play, but a shrewd fear of punishment, and a strategic submission to obey.

The question for Christians is this: is God a monolithic all-powerful will to which we must submit or the one who is a triune relationship of holy love, inviting us into a creative friendship?

Religions of holy wars and submission to God's will answer this question in one way; the way of the cross, forgiveness, and reconciliation answer it in another. In the former framework, fear motivates us to obedience based on the threat of punishment. In the Christian framework, fear does not signify the threat of punishment, but signifies the trembling awe of a sinner in the presence of holiness. It is an appropriate fear, not of a cowardice or a submission based on threat, but of a lover of truth who feels guilt and unworthiness in the presence of perfect love.

In the Christian frame, there is an honest fear based on my awareness of guilt. That is, it troubles me that I have not loved my neighbour or my God as I was intended. The good news declares that my fear based on guilt is interrupted by love. And so my anxiety about judgement meets the surprise of grace. Atonement casts out my fear of punishment. But guilt has played its part. In fact, had I lacked a sense of guilt, I would have no conscience. I would be dangerous indeed, with no capacity to feel guilty should I trespass across your life. Guilt-free, my one fear would be fear of getting caught and punished. Without a sense of fear as I stand guilty before the reality of holiness, there would be no psychological context for a sinner to experience gratitude for amazing grace.

The Path of Obedience

If fear is cast out by perfect love, how shall we interpret the Christian teaching that the path of obedience is a key signpost of the journey into love?: 'If you love me, obey my commandments' (John 14. 21). Do we not feel a great resistance and anger at those who call us to obey their will on threat of punishment? Is there a motive for obeying which is constructive, not a fear-ridden submission to a dominating authority?

The answer is that biblical obedience is far removed from obedience to anyone who happens to be powerful enough to issue orders. Hitler was a great advocate of obedience to the authority and law of the Third Reich. But despite times of confusion, the minority Confessing Church refused this call for submission because there was a growing awareness that obeying Jesus Christ is the opposite of submitting to a principle of will to power.

Clearly, there is a kind of obedience which wears us out, which motivates through threat and intimidation. This obedience springs from fear of punishment. Bruno Bettelheim noted from his two years in Dachau and Buchenwald, that students of World War II have often asked the question why did the Jews not revolt and fight against the Nazis? Especially in the concentration camps, why such acquiescence, why so few episodes of rebellion? Bettelheim's answer is that the rebels and fighters had by and large either fled the country or been killed in the attempt. Those who remained behind were either living in denial of the human capacity for evil or had become already so emotionally defeated that their concentration camp compliance was an obedience of fear, of hopelessness, with no self-respect but utter demoralization.[6]

Biblical obedience inhabits an utterly different atmosphere, the climate of God's generosity. 'God always gives before he commands', said Bonhoeffer.[7] We love because he first loved us. We have faith because he first valued and trusted, that is had faith, in us. We listen to God because he first listened to our cries for rescue. The root meaning of obedience is simply 'to hear'. God hears the cries of his lost sheep. We learn from his mercy and faithfulness to hear his voice, to imitate his inner character in our living. Biblical obedience is creative and not the opposite of freedom because it dwells in agreement with God's being as holy love. The syntax of obedience is determined by the semantics of love. To obey the way of agape is to work in harmony with the creative and loving centre of the Creator's purposes. To disobey agape is to revolt against life.

Jesus obeys his Father not in order to appease his Father's anger or divert it onto himself like some first-century Prometheus. His obedience reveals the inner heart of the Father's attitude and intention towards sinners. Without this identity of affection between Father and Son, the cross contradicts itself. It makes the Son's attitude of compassion the exact opposite of the Father's attitude of anger and the need to punish someone. But the cross reveals in the Son the Father's sprint down the road to embrace the prodigal. Jesus reveals God's intention to bridge the chasm between our darkness and his love. To become a Christian means to discover that God is the loving Father disclosed by his only begotten Son. I now can learn to abandon all motives for obedience based on the distorted notion that God's attitude to sinners is either indifference or a preference to punish.

Cowering obedience has not heard the gospel. The new obedience, the new hearing, reflects the discovery that God sent his son, not to condemn, but to rescue and restore. An obedience born of love releases in me a flow of activity and emotion which is unfrustrated by fear of evaluation and rejection. God's good will is not to bully us into submission by filling us with fears which block our hearts. His love sets us free to love as he loves, without domineering, without smothering.

The logic of biblical obedience is this: in our twisted enslavement to sin, God hears our cry for deliverance. Our reply to his hearing our cry is obedience. Obedience reveals our learning to internalize and integrate his compassion and holiness within our lives in response to his having first heard us. When we are energized by the nurturing love of Christ, not by fear, obedience is not a burden. Obedience frees us to do what is right and true in the face of every other impulse we may experience: 'the lust of the flesh, the lust of the eye, the pride of life' (1 John 5.3). Who does not obey what he truly loves?

As parents and teachers, how shall we re-learn with our children an obedience which springs from love not fear? An obedience which internalizes the skills and disciplines of creative order and commitment is vitally important in all fields of worthwhile endeavour. Pity the child who experiences no discipline at home. Pity the child who diets on a discipline of intimidation, shaming, and other strategies of fear. The worst of both worlds occurs in a home where a confused and confusing oscillation between these takes place.

I struggle here for I am not a perfect parent, nor did I have perfect parents. The discipline I pass on is tainted with 'fear which has to do with punishment'. As a rule of thumb, I have discovered that as a parent I am prone to use the tactics of intimidation or shaming at a point of similarity with my own childhood. I lose my temper and abuse the weak in situations not unlike those in which my father lost his. When I feel that someone is dominating me by their moods, I understand that I am reacting not only at them, but at those times reaching all the way back to childhood when I felt controlled and pressured by others. It is not startling to discover that we have little control over these responses. But we may begin to practise stepping to the side and acknowledge by name the awkward angle where the conflict is causing stress. We can take the time to reflect on the fact that here an old wound has been reopened. The practice of confession is my greatest tool in provoking a turning-point in which I cease passing on the wound. But if we do not explore both the meaning of this wound and therefore alternative ways to proceed, we merely pass our sins to the next generation. He who today is intimidated tomorrow slides into the role of intimidator. On the other hand, the docile and submissive child may repeat that role as a parent, thus enabling the child to dominate and control them and so replaying a familiar tune. Fear of falling off the subservient side of the horse may cause a parent to fall over on the opposite side of harsh control.

Suppose one's six-year-old refuses to eat the meal which has been prepared or refuses to go upstairs when it is bedtime. Suppose the parent begins to feel panic, anxiety and anger. A tender spot has been touched. Over the months and years, after one has exhausted the various intimidating possibilities, scolding, shouting, shaming, spanking, and so on, and one is weary of the resulting obedience out of fear and shame, which will turn either to self-hate or parent-hate some day, one can in a spirit of adventure begin to explore ever so awkwardly a new way. Instead of chiding and nagging, one can wonder what might be going on in the child? We take the risk of summoning the inquiring, childlike part of ourselves to a dialogue with our own child. By our openness, we will invite them to 'cast their cares upon us' instead of labelling their behaviour 'naughty'. For example: 'What's wrong with bathing and going to bed?', 'Too tired', 'You look tired. Very soon you can have a rest.' Suppose we calmly explain the reasons for bath and bed as an advocate, not a prosecutor: 'We bathe and sleep so our bodies and minds stay healthy. So let us finish this final job, so we can both rest. I am feeling tired too.' From her collapse into a foetal position in the middle of the floor, father gently but firmly lifts her. And lo, without scolding or threats, the child wearily trudges up the stairs.

Successful rapport is rarely permanent. Disobedience may be more serious than refusing to prepare for bed. But if God has put it into our hearts to teach discipline which springs from love, then in spite of stops and stutters, we pilgrim in search of a discipline which gracefully reflects God's own. Should you begin to experience this transition in your own efforts at parenting, you may enter your home with a new, unwelcome, awareness. It is a sense of sadness over how little love we have left to give upon arrival. Along the way we shall grieve to find not a few places where our own discipline has evolved from fear and shame. We shall grieve to be brought up short in the discovery of how impatient, intolerant, and limited is our capacity to love. But the alternatives could be put as starkly as this: obedience from fear breeds mistrust and discourages us into depression as we fight off the guilt and fear of disapproval; obedience from love creates belief and confidence and encourages us on our journey.

Yes, in my tiredness and need, I am a natural target for impatience and irritability. When I indulge this tendency, it is easy then to start scolding myself, in fact to start treating myself the same way I feel like treating, or have already treated, the others. At this frantic moment I need to hear and allow the gospel to interrupt my downward spiral, allow it to bear upon me in my darkness and acknowledge that here in this terribly familiar situation is a time and a place in which I hunger, thirst, and mourn for a love and a grace which I do not possess. Within this moment of mourning, I can call a halt to my crusade against sin and be able to embrace and not curse sinners, including myself. In these moments of awareness and mourning of my limits, the love of Christ shines upon an old, experienced sinner, releasing new energy to reach out to young, inexperienced sinners not with eagle-eyed condemnation but quick-eyed compassion.

Sinners in Recovery: Love and Law

It is not coincidental that the Epistle of John contains at once the strongest warning against sin alongside the greatest of tenderness toward sinners. Repeatedly, this letter refers to readers as 'my little children', unafraid to repetitively use the diminutive of affection juxtaposed with the gravest warnings against sin, which he characterizes as lawlessness (1 John 3.4). How different from our recurrent inclination to administer discipline as though we are sergeants training the military. John knows from within that the source of true discipline is the manner of love of the Father. He lives within that security. He wants his readers to live within it as well, especially when for love's sake he warns us regarding the consequences of sin.

This diminutive of personal affection is the distinguishing mark of Christian ethics and nurture. John hardly takes sin lightly: 'My dear children, I write this to you so that you will not sin' (2.1); 'Any one who does not do what is right is not a child of God; nor is anyone who does not love his brother' (3.10b); 'If anyone has material possessions and sees his brother in need but has no pity on him, how can the love of God be in him?'(3.17). But he bonds together the strongest opposition towards sin with tenderness to sinners. John repeatedly reminds us that we are God's children, not because we are mature and obedient, but because of the great love which the Father has lavished upon us (3.1).

Perhaps the great danger of the Church, which takes the threat of sin with full seriousness, is to forget the 'my little children' and only feel the weight of 'I write that you sin not'. It is God's love which creates the good law, not the opposite. Where law and obedience are torn away from God's gracious love, we sever holiness from grace. We project a god into heaven of a domineering authority who we fear for all the wrong reasons, who keeps us in a permanent state of anxious, obedient alert. The result is either an army of inflated, self-righteous crusaders, or deflated 'prisoner-of-war-camp' obeisance where a certain number eventually become 'absent-without-leave' prodigals.

Love and firmness are not opposites. Nor does love mean that law has no proper role to play. In *The Silver Chair*, the children Jill and Scrubb disobey Aslan. He had given four signs to guide them in their quest to rescue the prince. He reminds them to repeat these signs twice a day and trust them because in the adventure they would not appear in any way they could anticipate. Soon Jill becomes so preoccupied with her adventures (the plot), she forgets to repeat the signs (the theme). She forgets them altogether. Her disobedience leads to a near fatal encounter with the evil giants. So how shall Aslan recover his disobedient adventurers? Shall he burst into their prison, roaring? Shall he punish by letting them fail in their task? Instead, he comes quietly in a dream (which Jill could choose to ignore). He appears to her, telling her to repeat the signs. She of course has forgotten them. 'At that, a great horror came over her. And Aslan took her up in his jaws (she could feel his lips and his breath but not his teeth) and carried her to the window' to see the signs once again.[8] The next day, when escape is possible, she remembers the directions Aslan has shown her through the window in her dream. The judgement upon her disobedience is that her quest will be more difficult, her success delayed. But the quest is not abandoned. Jill is not rejected. Perfect love casts out fear and draws us on to a true love for listening to the signs and remembering them. The lion is at once firm and gentle. 'Aslan took her up in his jaws. She could feel his lips and his breath, but not his teeth.'

There are many reasons we forget the signs, that is, disobey God's holy laws. Some do so out of a reaction to an obedience based on fear. But there is a new world of God's holy love which evokes in us a desire to obey his commands. In this dominion we discover that conditions of acceptance are transposed into responses to grace. The discipline of prayer has become not an obligation to fulfil, but the knowledge that the Father's love grants permission for us to delight in uncluttered space and time to enjoy and explore with God what it is he has been doing in us and what further signs shall be given for us to learn or recover. Prayer becomes that gracious invitation a Christian finds where 'one may without much molestation, be thinking what he is, whence he came, what he has done, and to what the King has called him'.[9]

In the glad obedience of prayer I hear the Father tell me I am free to relish his presence as Mary did without Martha's need to do things for him, without exhausting myself and other people, neglecting my family in the fearful obedience of endless and repetitive achievements, successes, and the anxious need to earn more praise. The new world of the Father's love grants me time to obey his call to enter his sabbath, to be refreshed in his love, to have space to become at peace with him in the quiet. Hereafter, as we wield the gospel plough, our labour shall toil within prayer's calm climate. The spirit of children at play before the Father smiles as much as our body sweats. Our obedience and toil shall not be humourless and driven, but edged with the awareness that love freely reaches out to us here and now because love has run down the road towards the prodigal, wept at the gates of Jerusalem, borne the cross to Golgotha, walked to Emmaus, and eaten fish over charcoals with Peter the denier. And this love now comes to break bread with us and summons us to an obedience grounded in grace. Such commands are not burdensome. Who does not obey what he truly loves, and who truly loves him? 'Come to me, all you who are weary and heavy laden, and I will give you rest. Take my yoke upon you and learn from me, for I am gentle and humble in heart, and you will find rest for your souls. For my yoke is easy and my burden is light' (Matt. 11.28-30).

Wearing the yoke of obedience, and discovering the freedom of prayer's discipline, are signs that we have travelled far since we began considering how the redemption of hate weans us from fear. These are hopeful discoveries along the journey of love's development. A further labour of love's maturing awaits us.

Notes

1 John Calvin, *The Institutes of the Christian Religion*, (Eng. trans., Philadelphia: Westminster Press, 1975; Latin original, 1559, Book One, iii, 1), p. 43.

2 John Sutherland, *Fairbairn's Journey into the Interior*, (London: Free Association Books, 1989), pp. 59, 111, 129f. No discussion of this topic would be complete without mentioning the seminal work of Ian Suttie, *The Origins of Love and Hate*, (London: Kegan Paul, [1935], 1948), p. 208. Fairbairn had read and absorbed the importance of Suttie. cf. Sutherland, p. 118.

3 Christopher Blumhardt, *Thy Kingdom Come, A Blumhardt Reader*, ed. Vernard Eller, (Grand Rapids: Eerdmans), p. 132.

4 Quoted in John Powell, *The Secret of Staying in Love*, (Illinois: Argus, 1974), p. 20.

5 Georges Bernanos, *The Diary of a Country Priest*, (New York: Doubleday, [1937], 1959), p. 130.

6 Bruno Bettelheim, *The Informed Heart*, (New York: The Free Press, [1960], 1961), p. 293ff.

7 Dietrich Bonhoeffer, *Ethics*, (New York: Macmillan, [1949], 1973), p. 151.

8 C. S. Lewis, *The Silver Chair*, (London: Puffin, [1953], 1979), p. 104.

9 John Bunyan, *Pilgrim's Progress*, (London: Ward Lock and Co.), p. 248 (part 2, The Comfort and Peace of the Valley).

8

Via Dolorosa

Without a doubt the experience of suffering, whether personally or on a large social scale, is the great barrier to belief that God is love. If God is all-powerful love, why does he let a young mother die of cancer or whole regions starve to death? Did Christianity develop to provide a religious answer to this problem? If it did, it has made a poor job of it. It is more accurate to say that Christianity creates the problem of suffering rather than solves it with a respectable religious solution. Unless I already believe in an all-powerful God of love, a tragic experience may jolt me, but why should it surprise me more than any other event, followed in a random chain by something pleasant, but perhaps something worse? Apart from a loving God, suffering is one more chance event. What else did I expect?

Then why inflict this belief on ourselves if it creates such a problem? First, because with or without a God of love, I still live in a world with many tragedies which I must seek to make sense of, even if I conclude it is all nonsense. But fundamentally a believer in Jesus reckons that Christian faith accounts for the presence of sacrificial love which has made all the difference in healing many tragic situations. It particularly makes sense of the history of Israel, of Jesus, and of the Church's witness to the nations. The fact is that it is impossible to discuss the meaning of love without the path of suffering being acknowledged as inseparably near by.

An Intimate Coexistence

It soon becomes evident that in the Bible, agape and suffering have an intimate coexistence. There are large hints that the very act of creation itself, springing as it does from love, involves suffering. To create God had to stare both at the threatening curse and the threatening misery and in the face of these utter the words, 'Let there be . . .'. Late in life, C. S. Lewis muses that: 'Perhaps there is an anguish, an alienation, a crucifixion involved in the creative act.'[1] On the mundane level of everyday creativity, Rollo May has written that every act of creativity demands courage to encounter and form something new. This always entails risk: our lives may be changed by the new forms, patterns, symbols, or by the new society we may build. There will be opposition by those with vested interest in the status quo in art, science, religion, and politics.[2] The New Testament displays an awareness that within the drama of creation, costly sacrifice is close by when it describes Jesus as the lamb 'slain before the foundation of the world' (1 Pet. 1.20). We know redemption is costly. That creation itself anticipates this costliness verifies the intrinsic connection between love and suffering, a connection that consists of varying levels of intensity.

Consider our capacity for loving relationships in the light of attachment theory. Should a child encounter even the threat of separation, anxiety and fear of loss naturally arise, inspiring him to do whatever is necessary to stay connected. This built-in response to fear of loss or non-attachment does not disappear with passing years. Within love relationships there is an inherent awareness of vulnerability to pain and loss. If we apply this to the inner harmony of the triune God, it hardly suggests that agape goes looking for pain. Jesus did not go to the cross out of some masochistic need to suffer. He frankly asked not to go. But agape values the beloved so profoundly that it shall traverse whatever pain is necessary to reunite the beloved object to itself. Hence to love is to suffer.

St Paul names this intimate connection between love and suffering when he writes 'love is longsuffering and kind' (1 Cor. 13.4). If I look at life with a 'television advertisement' perspective and view things and people as existing to service my needs, the idea of suffering love seems a grotesquely unwelcome suggestion. It certainly will not enhance the sales of most consumer items. But if life is, in Bunyan's words, a 'dangerous journey' not a luxury cruise, that is, a series of conflicts and challenges, then confronting difficulties will bring pain and sorrow as well as joy and celebration. St Paul's analogy of the Christian running a race to win the prize reminds us that an athlete in training strains, stretches, and endures pain in order to win a race (1 Cor. 9.24). If a runner does not exercise, his muscles are not in any fit condition. He becomes short of breath and cannot hope to win. If I do not face my problems, if I ignore, procrastinate, and blame others, I will store up a mountain of unresolved problems for myself. All of us to some degree avoid our problems and hence the suffering they bring us. But to that extent we are less fit in body and in spirit. Our capacity for love diminishes. We risk being unable to run the race and fight the good fight.

The Comforts of Love?

Despite the deep ties linking love and suffering, it is not just the Marxist who has noticed how religion can often be recruited to help us avoid our problems and pains. Most of us know in some inner, hungry place the appeal of the travelling preacher who tells us in stirring testimonial that if only we would fully believe in his message, his programme or his snake oil, we will experience victorious living. But William Penn knew better when he uttered his Quaker epithet: 'No cross, no crown.' Love energizes us to face the tragic and to strengthen our spirits, not to avoid, but to wrestle with difficulties. Love suffers long. Is this a shabby reward for love? If life is a pilgrimage, not a resort cruise, then the power to be patient and long-suffering may be our most precious gift. Perhaps we should identify love not so much with the comfort it brings, but with the courage it provides to embrace the unavoidable trials and tribulations which life presents. Sometimes a parent may try too hard to alleviate the suffering of a complaining child. The more they try to cheer him up, the more the child complains. Why? He does not feel they appreciate the extent of his sufferings. But in honouring the difficulty of his situation they rouse energy to help him endure. Comfort comes later, after love recovers the energy formerly wasted in avoiding suffering and becomes available for constructive living which honestly faces our difficulties.

Whenever we lose a loved-one or leave behind a part of our life we have loved, the process of saying a 'good'-bye and letting go produces the peculiar suffering which we call mourning. Yet Jesus tells us those who experience mourning are blessed. It is good to grieve for thereby we honour the people and places who have nurtured and valued us and from whom we are now separated. To avoid or neglect the task of mourning may be a sign of cowardice in the face of suffering.

When love requires suffering, the refusal to suffer is the refusal to love. But this does not mean suffering is avoided. It creates instead an unhealthy, unredemptive suffering. As Carl Jung observes: 'Neurosis is always a substitute for legitimate suffering.'[3] The substitute becomes more painful than the suffering we try to avoid. We laugh with the wry humour of recognition at the panic and trauma which the television character Basil Fawlty suffers because rather than admit to an error or apologize he chooses to tell a series of increasingly complex lies. He goes through hell and takes others with him rather than lose face. Love names our avoidances, our fear of losing face, and empowers us with the humility to face our problems and suffer the necessary pains of working with them.

It is revealing to contrast agape's response to suffering with that of eros. Eros says, 'I must have this now. I cannot wait. I am lost without her' or whatever it is for which we long. Because eros demands satisfaction now, it is not patient. It cannot endure for very long. I am not saying that eros does not suffer, however. When in the grip of eros, we often experience great anguish when we do not receive promptly what we desire. But eros on its own has no enduring and sustaining quality. Marriages centred on eros can be short and not very sweet. Eros's desire for satisfaction and fulfilment leads us into marriage and can as forcefully lead us out–with betrayal and rejection. When marriages endure, and not just as a shell, it is because a death to eros occurs in order that a larger love may be reborn from its ashes. Love experiences the pain of cherishing the non-ideal as I embrace the imperfect child, church, or partner which real life has brought into my pathway. Agape perseveres in non-romantic, unattractive situations. Only agape has the strength to endure even crucifixion for the sake of the beloved.

The Divine Pattern

The presence of agape rarely eliminates suffering directly. It may even temporarily heighten our suffering. Love may provide strength to endure suffering rather than eradicate it. If love is supposed to eliminate suffering then at Jesus's trial in the wilderness, the ministering angels' timing was a bit off. More likely did their ministry strengthen him for the renewed certainty that what had begun must be endured and indeed would be overcome. Jesus suffers on the cross (and not only on the cross) not so we may never have to endure pain and death, an especially appealing notion of redemption, but in order that our suffering may become like his, that is, in some small but genuine way, both creative and redemptive. In Hebrews 5.8 we are told that suffering is essential to the process by which Jesus reclaims and untwists our distorted humanity. How likely is it that his followers would be permitted to side-step the master's clear pathway in this regard? To choose to love will lead us into suffering and lead us to where other people suffer.

St Paul goes so far as to perceive a blessed chain reaction in suffering's role in our redemption:

> We rejoice in our sufferings, knowing that suffering produces endurance, and endurance produces character, and character produces hope and hope does not disappoint us, because God's love has been poured into our hearts through the Holy Spirit which has been given to us. (Rom. 5.3–5)

Is St Paul naive? Does he not realize that suffering usually produces rather negative consequences such as discouragement, doubt and despair? St Paul's inner logic is born from his own experience which severed the old chain reaction. He too had inherited the view that suffering is a punishment, and thus an embarrassment and a scandal, something best avoided by earning righteousness, success, and security through piety and a hard-work ethic. He too was once offended at the suggestion that God had died on a cross between two thieves.

The foundation of St Paul's new logic is his discovery in the Holy Spirit that 'while we were yet helpless, at the right time Christ died for the ungodly' (v. 6). That is, God's suffering and death 'for us' has transfigured St Paul's attitude toward and experience of suffering. Its stigma as curse is shared and borne by Christ. Its humiliating label now becomes God's signature written in blood that he is our redeemer. In the wake of the cross, suffering must be reconsidered. And it confirms what was hinted at in the Old Testament, which Joseph discovered in the dungeon after his brothers sold him into slavery, after Potiphar threw him into prison, and which he declared to his brothers, 'You meant it for evil, but God meant it for good' (Gen. 50.20). It verifies what Moses experienced far away from the glory of Egypt, having fled to the desert for his crime of murder, where in exile and humiliation God speaks to him from a burning bush. It is possible not to resent and despise suffering or seek to flee it, but with the lenses of the cross, to inquire into its meaning and purpose, sometimes angrily, always passionately.

Frederick Buechner portrays the change in the way Christian faith approaches suffering by pondering the great symbols of world religions–a splendid six-pointed star, a lovely crescent moon, a captivating lotus flower, and . . . a cross, symbol of torture and execution. It certainly interrupts our normal habits of religious piety. At the least it gives one pause for hope.[4] The identification of shame and disgrace with suffering are replaced with the hope of glory and the promise of perfection through what we suffer for righteousness' sake. That God accompanies us in our suffering rather than abandons us to it begins a sea change in our experience and thinking about suffering and about God. As Dorothy Sayers reminds us, the incarnation teaches that 'for whatever reason God chose to make man as he is–limited and suffering and subject to sorrows and death–He had the honesty and the courage to take his own medicine'.[5]

Even when agape meets us most profoundly at our point of suffering, love never devalues the importance of our response to suffering nor makes our reaction irrelevant in the healing process. Consider the healing of the man who lay crippled by the pool of Bethzatha in the fifth chapter of John's Gospel. His first response to Jesus's question, 'Do you want to be healed?' is defensive: 'Sir, I have no man to put me into the pool when the water is troubled, and while I am going another steps down before me.' Rather than answer the question, he offers an alibi for why he has not been healed. Probably less impolite than anxious to assuage his guilt, he no doubt assumes that Jesus, like the others, blames this illness and the resultant suffering on some personal sin in his life. People who are unwell usually feel rather disapproved of and guilty for being ill. In folk religions old and new, ill health is synonymous with the gods' disapproval. Our resulting guilt feelings within and rejection from without provoke us to create elaborate explanatory systems for our present illness. Our defensive efforts rarely convince others and only succeed in siphoning off our energy, injecting lethargy into our spirits. The spiralling burden of our guilt and our anxiety to defend against it snuffs out hope and may even cut the nerve of any desire to get well.

Over a prolonged stretch of adversity, suffering and disappointment can so empty us of energy that we lose any will to live. We
resent and are weary of life. Especially are we weary of and well
defended against glib religious solutions. So powerful and disabling
is this experience of world-weariness amidst suffering that sloth,
or *accidie*, has been interpreted by those acquainted with it as
the strongest passion of all, stronger than lust, more paralysing
than pride. It feels as if there is no use trying. We shrug our
shoulders, recite our excuses, and wait with melancholy for the
angels who never seem to show.

Not an Ideal Rescue

Suffering also tempts us to indulge ourselves with fantasies of
how our rescue should occur. The angelic display of troubling
the water with holy bubbles seems an essential prerequisite to
the real presence of God's healing power: 'If only the mystical
encounter with the angel comes, I shall be healed.' Of course,
there is a de-mythologized, 'honest-to-God' version of the same
expectation: 'If only a new job or a new, marvellous friend or a
new place to live would enter my life, then all would be well.'
Meanwhile, I lie listless by the pool, put my life permanently on
hold, and wait for someone or something angelic to come and
make me happy. In this timelessness of 'meanwhile' I also find
all manner of things and people to resent. I not only blame
angelic incompetence, but my friends, my church, and my neighbours for not helping me to get into the pool at the appropriate
moment. 'If only I had four friends like the paralytic had. I'll be
lucky to have four pall-bearers.'

We may sedate ourselves during our suffering by fantasizing
about our future rescue, snuggling into an imagined cocoon of
tomorrow's release. There is no denying that religion has been
used as an opiate to take our hurting minds off the pain. One
way to investigate whether my beliefs are suffering from truth
decay is to ask whether my faith helps me face the real problems
which my community and I are suffering or whether it encourages me to withdraw from the difficult and the tragic. To sing
about my rescue while keeping a safe distance from feeding
the hungry, helping the homeless, and visiting the sick and the
prisoner, exposes the sweet tooth of a religious addiction.

Such fantasies may close me off from the real healing and

healer when the fullness of time is at hand. Seen from this perspective, Jesus's summons to get up and walk creates a knife-edge
of heaven and hell. The paralytic must find something left within
himself which is not utterly committed to his ideal healing of
angels, bubbly water, and competent friends, something which
can trust this personal call to do the very thing he knows he
cannot do: 'Pick up your mat and walk.'

Notice that in this command, Jesus addresses the illness head
on. One way of helping people cope with suffering is to take
their minds off their problem by identifying and helping to
develop their strengths. Positive thinking and encouraging our
strengths surely assist us when we are stuck in persistent problems.
But real limits come when we face the sheer absence of potential
for change, the long-standing deprivation, or the prolonged vic-
timization. What do you build on to see when you are blind?
Why look for ways to balance nutrition when you are starving?
At such moments Jesus simply faces the tragic facts, confronting
them fairly and squarely.

Not a Philosophy of Optimism

We must be wary how we translate St Paul's admonition to rejoice
in our suffering. It is perpetually tempting to render his words
into a philosophy of optimism. Optimism takes Paul's testimony
out of its intersection with the cross of Jesus and waves it as a
magic attitude-wand at the tragic side of life. Instead of weeping
with those who weep, positive thinking not only prematurely
provides comfort by urging us to rejoice, but implicitly scolds us
for weeping. In the eighteenth century the 'best of all possible
worlds' became a glib recipe which the affluent and self-confident
used to reassure themselves, suffocate their doubts, and shame
the suffering into falling in step. In the past decade a rash of
positive thinking has made something of a political revival,
seeking to utilize the energy of optimism to promote consumer
confidence while blaming and shaming those who experience
failure and suffering. So the family with good jobs, healthy children, fire in the hearth, and money for a holiday, can switch
on the television and watch the homeless, the hungry, and the
dole queues, safely and peacefully at a distance, within their
own sitting-rooms. We sigh and are grateful for 'there but for the
grace of God go I'.

Such gratitude has a formal affinity to Christian faith but actually passes by on the other side like the pharisee and the priest in Jesus's parable. It refuses or is incapable of weeping with those who weep. It does not ask the question of compassion, 'What must I do to help?' but only suggests people try harder or stop their bad habits, or makes some other exhortation. For example: 'Perhaps you should lie closer to the pool in case the angels come? Why not make yourself a bit more presentable and cultivate some friendships so you will have better help?' Moralistic optimism noisily exhorts the sufferer to buck up, subtly scolds him for his predicament, and blames the intensity of his difficulties on the error of his attitudes or perhaps his forebears: 'Who sinned, this man or his parents?' (John 9.2). Such a theory provides no hope and only contributes to the sufferer's rage or depression. It deserves the ridicule of Voltaire's *Candide* in any century.

The call of Jesus to the cripple has no rebuke or blame. It builds not on his untapped strength but only on the compassion of God. Only because the true crisis is not minimized but addressed, only because there is clearly no confusing of the focus of who to trust in, only because the questioner speaks with love, will the suffering man have the choice to hear and believe this compassionate call and distinguish it from the routine condescension of good advice and moral optimism.

When God comes to his wounded creation, does he say 'yes' only to the natural optimism of bright colours, pleasing shapes, successes, and energetic achievements but 'no' to our sorrow, our humiliation, our pain, or our failure? No way. He says 'yes' to our humanity, embraces our flesh, becomes one of us, experiencing our greatness and our wretchedness (Pascal), yet without sin. The contrasts of joy and sorrow are not alien to the man of sorrows. He does not spare himself both the menace and the hope of creation. Creation is so valued that God wills to embrace the contradictions of creaturely life. He calls us to weep with those who weep because he has first wept. It is only the one who openly weeps at the grave of Lazarus who dares to cry out in hope beyond human possibilities, 'Lazarus, come forth!' God's 'no' to sin uniquely confronts the power of evil, but not by avoiding evil or by assimilating it into a catch-all philosophy which in effect denies its seriousness.

In the Presence of Death

Jesus Christ conquered death. He did not escape it. To those left
behind, death leaves a legacy of unparalleled pain. How can the
loss which death delivers ever be healed? In grieving the loss of
his wife, C. S. Lewis records how the more desperately he needed
God's comfort, the less he felt him.[6] The trained ear of John
Bowlby, the renowned psychiatrist, hears in the enormity of
Lewis's pain and sense of God's utter absence, an unmistakeable
echo of the trauma which Lewis the nine-year-old boy suffered
in losing his mother to cancer, and the utterly inadequate support for him in his efforts at mourning this loss.[7] This early and
unresolved grief hugely amplified the adult loss of his wife. But
Lewis's honest and outspoken grieving which he permitted himself
as an adult surely facilitated the healing he was not permitted
when as a child he was whisked away to boarding-school by a dis-
consolate father, himself unapproachable and further separated
from his sons by the pain of his own loss. Nor did the school
provide a safe, listening ear to bring his grief.

Had Lewis not written with painful honesty the extent of his
suffering at his wife's loss, it is doubtful he could have experienced the quality of hope described in the final pages of the
book. Even so, the candour and starkness of his anguish led him
to publish the book under a pseudonym, lest his honest grappling
scandalize those shocked to read how a well-known Christian
would agonize so intensely over his wife's death. Certainly the
comfort he was offered and which he describes contrasts greatly
with the expectations one might have for a 'great Christian'.
Absent are the waves of liquid love that gave Charles Finney
comfort during his traumatic conversion: 'There was no sudden,
striking and emotional transition.' What progress from the
bottom he records is much more 'like the warming of a room or
the coming of daylight. When you first notice them they have
already been going on for some time'.[8]

In the end, no logic, no dazzling experience brings consola-
tion. As Luther understood, who himself knelt and wept bitterly
at the bedside of two dying daughters, only he who inflicts and
permits the wounds is able also to heal them. No one else. Should
our own faith collapse under the unrelenting presence of pain,
even so hope is not destroyed, for our hope is that we are up-
held even in our weakness and lack of faith by Another. Let us
not be too embarrassed by Lewis's or Luther's tears in the face

of the loss of their loved ones, nor too surprised when our own are added. It is not part of our witness to the resurrection to minimize the immensity of our losses at death. The sole comfort Lewis received he connects closely to the presence of the suffering redeemer; the shining tears of the great lion in *The Magician's Nephew*. The only comfort we can take from honestly facing the tomb must be closely linked to Jesus himself and the way he stood before the tomb of Lazarus, the way he reached into death itself, and despite its prodigious appearance, the way he spoke as if it must not have the final word.

In the Gospels, Jesus links the coming of death to the entering into a deeper life (Matt. 7.14). For St Paul, sharing in Christ's death is the meaning of Christian baptism. In the light of these realities, Luther, meditating upon death, wrote these words: 'Just as an infant is born with peril and pain from the small abode of its mother's womb into this immense heaven and earth, that is, into this world, so man departs this life through the narrow gate of death.' And though our present experience of earth and sky seems large enough, Luther reckons they are as a mother's womb in comparison with the future God prepares for those whom he loves. Preparing to die is preparing for one's new birth: the narrow tunnel, the labour period of intense pain, and then, breathing the new air of the kingdom.[9] All this is prologue to a fullness of life that eye has not seen and ear has not heard. We cannot convince anyone still in the womb of the joy which draws near. Birth itself makes such arguments irrelevant. But for those of us still in creation's womb, we do see Jesus 'crowned with glory and honour because of the suffering of death, so that by the grace of God he might taste death for everyone' (Heb. 2.9).

God's Response to Suffering

Fair enough then, facing suffering enables me to mature. Accepting my limits lets me feel the gift of life more deeply as blessing. Learning to live with my limitations frees me to celebrate the honest joys and sorrows of bodily life: 'Go eat your bread with joy and drink your wine with a glad heart; for what you do God has approved beforehand' (Eccles. 9.7). But there comes a moment of trial, the final straw, where the affliction is such that we doubt God can use this suffering. Confidence is shredded. Here is precisely where Christian faith reveals that

God himself is personally impaled on the horns of the dilemma of suffering: 'Only he who inflicts and permits the wounds is able also to heal them. No one else.' For Christians, Jesus's crucifixion discloses the problem of suffering in its most intense and agonizing instance. It describes how God himself came as a man, was falsely tried, tortured and executed. This God who became 'a man of sorrows and acquainted with grief' (Isa. 53.3) not only intensifies but is caught up in the problem of suffering. As we hear his story, perhaps we do not find nor are meant to find an intellectual answer that restores conceptual control, but we may instead discover the grace of love at work within the sufferings of our own life, the lives of others, and the very life of God.

We have seen how suffering seduces us to withdraw into isolation with our pain, and to idealize certain kinds of rescue. In our resulting paralysis, we are unable to respond to a word of freedom, which summons us to get up and walk with no guarantees of how our rescue shall be accomplished *sans* bubbles and angels. Inner paralysis is every bit as inhibiting to the cripple's healing as his physical incapacities. Suffering can so dry up our soul that not a seed of hope can take root and be nourished. In desperation we wait for magic bubbles that ask nothing of us and call none of our assumptions into question.

At such moments we are deaf to the word of hope. We feel the ultimate absence of all that is good. We imagine ourselves, as Simone Weil has described it, to be the greatest possible distance from love.[10] We feel that we have been hammered by a nail that pierces the very centre of our souls. What can possibly breach this hopelessness and isolation? The gospel of Jesus, the crucified God, says that over this supreme distance, this supreme tearing-apart that distances us from all love and hope, God has stretched his arms wide and embraced us. That is the cross. Something of an anticipatory stretching of love had to span that infinite distance within the weary soul of the paralytic. Only this non-coercive power of love could lift him up in such a way that his healing came through the free response of faith in love's invitation. This is that agonizing moment of grace when the afflicted soul encounters the choice to let go of his expectations for what will make his life whole, in the face of the personal Word who ministers to the sufferer according to 'the counsel of his own will' (Eph. 1.11). This Jesus, not the angels, speaks an invitation to restoration. He follows no prescribed methods, tells no one another's story.

Only a love which is willing to suffer with us can heal. We need a love which loves us when we are unattractive, when we are walled into our ugliness, when we are immersed in tragedy. Only a God willing to die for us, willing to descend into hell for us is of any help. A love connected only to the heights of ecstasy or the irresistibility of absolute power has no elasticity to stoop, no depth to endure tragedy without snapping and abandoning the once loved object. A god of spectacle and awesome displays of power cannot help when there is only brokenness and failure, when there is no audience to observe a marvellous miracle, when I am all alone in my sin. I have only one hope: a love which is unafraid to bear my sin, share my pain, and to be 'broken and wounded' for my transgression.

This is the love Jesus lived among us. This is the love that freed him to endure the cross. This is the love that has conquered even death. This is the love we are invited by Jesus to share with the world. Such love rarely makes the headlines, but its impact endures. No one loved like this stays the same. The height of God's power only unveils itself by the depth of his love on the cross. Perhaps only those recognize the power of love who have themselves experienced prisons of hate, self-pity, or pride and have discovered that in the cross they are not abandoned in their prisons, but loved. Yes, agape suffers long, but it heals.

In *The Magician's Nephew*, Aslan, the great lion, asks Digory to undo the wrong he has committed. He is asked to pluck an apple from the ice-encircled tree, with no guarantees of the consequences for his dying mother. By contrast, the witch at once prophesies, correctly, that the apple will cure his mother if he takes it straightaway, with the witch, back to London instead of to the lion. He has no similar promise from the lion. This tempts Digory to bargain with Aslan: 'I'll try to help you if you'll try to help about my mother.'[11] The witch later tempts him with a specific promise of physical healing whereas again the lion simply summons him to undo his wrongs, with no guarantees of the outcome. (The story is the more poignant for in Lewis's own childhood, his mother died of cancer, and in *Surprised by Joy*, he recalls how he prayed for healing and received no answer. As a result, he would soon abandon his childish Christianity of magic and bargaining.) Therefore instead of negotiating, he simply and straightforwardly asks Aslan for a cure for his mother. But the startling event that carries Digory across the aching fear of his mother's absence is the great shining tears in the lion's eyes. Later at the height of the witch's seduction, only the memory of those tears sustains him during the most unromantic moments of his task.

When you and I feel hammered by life, we hang alongside that love like the two thieves on either side of Jesus. Sometimes we hang there because it is our own fault. Sometimes it feels as though we have had lots of help. It is possible we may be so weighed down and broken by our personal cross that we fail to notice the One who hangs alongside. Witness the one thief who hung beside Jesus and mocked him. But the fact remains that because of his cross planted in history, the intolerable moment of my personal pain and isolation is neither perpetual nor final. Through the confusing throbs and dull ache, pierce the shining tears of God. The nails, the spears, and the jeers cannot carry out their threat to have the last word. The passion of Jesus stretches from the Father's everlasting 'yes' toward sinners to his utter 'no' toward evil. Such love is never poured into a void, but becomes the healing centre. Even my small corner is not abandoned, but is bound to that centre. My isolation is brought into the holy presence of the Trinity by the outstretched passion of the Son.

Suffering's final seduction is the temptation to make my torment the isolated, yet grandiose, pinnacle of all tragedy. But when I, not Digory, see God's tears, I am removed from my despairing but grand centrality and given the humbling presence of God himself suffering alongside. That infinite curse I feel like, the curse I feel like uttering, is gathered into Jesus's cry of dereliction to the Father. My isolation is breached by that cry, those tears, the outstretched hands.

Silence, both divine and human, appropriately follows such a disclosure. In stillness we absorb something of the enormity of this epiphany. But beyond the silence, away like thunder in the distance, the rumble of a cracking tombstone interrupts our darkest fridays with the roar of Easter.

> They shall hunger no more, neither thirst any more; the sun shall not strike them, nor any scorching heat. For the Lamb in the midst of the throne will be their shepherd, and he will guide them to springs of living water; and God will wipe away every tear from their eyes. (Rev. 7.16–17)

Notes

1 C. S. Lewis, *Letters to Malcolm*, (New York: Harcourt, 1963), p. 44.
2 Rollo May, *The Courage to Create*, (New York: Bantam, [1975], 1985), p. 15.
3 Carl Jung, 'Psychology and Religion, West and East', *Collected Works*, (Princeton: Princeton University Press, 1973), vol. II, p. 75.
4 Frederick Buechner, *Wishful Thinking*, (New York: Harper & Row, 1973), p. 19.
5 Dorothy L. Sayers, *Creed or Chaos*, (New York: Harcourt, 1949), p. 4.
6 C. S. Lewis, *A Grief Observed*, (London: Faber and Faber, [1961], 1968), p. 37.
7 John Bowlby, *Attachment and Loss*, (New York: Basic Books, 1980), vol. 3, p. 242.
8 C. S. Lewis, *A Grief Observed*, (London: Faber and Faber [1961], 1968), p. 49.
9 Martin Luther, 'A Sermon on Preparing to Die', *Collected Works*, (Philadelphia: Fortress Press, [1519], 1969), vol. 42, p. 99.
10 Simone Weil, *Waiting for God*, (New York: Harper, [1948], 1974), p. 124.
11 C. S. Lewis, *The Magician's Nephew*, (London: Puffin, [1955], 1978), p. 131.

9

Journey's End:
The Triumph of Love

Following Easter, believers, so far as we know, have never been
magically transported heavenward to celebrate the Supper of the
Lamb. We weep and rejoice in the history and dust of earth.
Nor in this present moment is the finality of Christ's triumph
clearly manifest. We still live in the 'not yet' of pride's old competitive warfare, yet nevertheless, despite evil's loud threats in
our time, each time we gather for word and sacrament we share
in an anticipatory feast of the kingdom, freely receiving of that
which is to come. As we do so, by faith the inward eye sees in our
midst the One who has interrupted the reign of evil, planting a
new domain.

The Old Enemy

The old dominion that boasts of its permanence and superiority
wears the banal label 'evil'. What do I mean by evil? All that
destroys life, all that is jealous, all that inflates me above or
deflates me below my neighbour, all that coldly withdraws from
my neighbour, all that impinges and seeks to control my neighbour. Evil can be active persecution or callous abandonment. It
may wish to harm. It may choose to pass by on the other side.
President Clinton's inaugural speech described it when he
warned that the American capital has become 'a place of intrigue
and calculation', where 'powerful people . . . worry endlessly
about who is in and who is out, who is up and who is down,
forgetting those people whose toil and sweat sends us here'. It is
the church meeting where an eloquent speaker, respecting all
due etiquette, speaks words, perhaps biblical words, occasionally
to wound or mock, but mostly to control, to arouse fear or to
be centre stage. Evil is ugly, cheap and petty. That is why it
veils itself as an angel of light, cloaking its cruelty in virtuous

vestments. Thus Simone Weil describes evil's enchantment which recruits us to its cause:

> Nothing is so beautiful, nothing is so continually fresh and surprising as the good; no desert is so dreary, monotonous and boring as evil. But with fantasy it's the other way round. Fictional good is boring and flat, while fictional evil is varied, intriguing, attractive and full of charm.[1]

Interestingly, Hannah Arendt reports that when a psychologist examined Adolf Eichmann, the Nazi war criminal who was responsible for the death of thousands, he was found to be sane.[2] The irony is that those who we regard with fear and who we stigmatize in our society are the mentally unstable or insane. Yet it is we the sane who are capable of the greatest evil. Somewhere Thomas Merton has written: 'It is the sane ones, the well adapted ones, who can without qualms and without nausea aim the missiles and press the buttons that will initiate the great festival of destruction, that they, the sane ones, have prepared.'

Evil thrives whenever we refuse to acknowledge our own sin but blame or project our disease on whoever or whatever reveals our deficiencies. The same self-justifying strategy afflicts institutions as well as individuals. The great irony of evil is that it is most active in whatever purports to be of ultimate importance. In areas of ultimate concern I most passionately identify myself with the highest and truest, and view my opponents as most worthy of contempt. Nowhere under heaven does self-righteousness thrive more than in religion. This is why the acknowledgement of evil, the confession of sin, personal and corporate, has a conspicuous place in Christian worship, for here I am learning to take responsibility for my sin. Here I am utterly cast upon grace to resolve the immensity of the problem. Here I learn to pray with David to stop covering up or excusing my trail of evil: 'Lord, cleanse me from my secret faults.' Here I learn with Jesus the enormous lesson, how to 'forgive those who trespass against us'.

Is evil a malignant, aggressive personal presence or simply a privation of good, a chaotic, indiscriminate emptiness? Such is the confusing nature of malice that both alternatives express stubborn facts. When we emphasize the personality of evil, and call it Satan, we borrow qualities of personhood and reality from the One who is good and who creates good, to describe a darkness which by its loveless schemes seeks to de-personalize and deaden. How contradictory to speak of a 'personal' devil when we hurl the qualities of personhood into a black hole of love's opposite! It becomes even more confusing to attempt a rational account of evil's origin and purposes, when they are essentially incoherent and corrupt. Theologies should be wary of glib explanations which minimize the fact that evil involves us in an emergency situation. How realistic is it to think that by direct inquiry into evil, evil would cast light on itself? The full meaning and malignity of evil is only unmasked by its assault upon love at the cross, and hence by love's chosen encounter with evil.

We have seen that the Bible offers no elaborate explanations of evil's origin. Like an uninvited guest at a party, like weeds sown in the night by an enemy (Matt. 13.25), evil sneaks in. God who is pure, uncreated light, cannot ignore evil or call it good. How shall he overcome it, especially as it threatens his good creation? Genesis describes how God separates light from darkness and blesses the light, calling it good. But, passing by the darkness, God rejects chaos and withholds his blessing from it. Later we are told that the Lord is utterly sovereign over the darkness (Isa. 45.5–7). Even it shall be used to praise him. Once and for all, it is in the Gospels that we see how the light of God lays claim even to the darkness for love's sake.

For let us be clear: nothing is more opposed to evil than agape. From the beginning, the Father of light implacably resists all evil and sin: 'God is light and in him there is no shadow of darkness' (1 John 1.5). Normally, opposition implies strident speeches, devastatingly militant campaigns, and coercive activity. But love's antagonism to evil is both more total and totally unlike such strategies. Love's 'no' to evil reaches back to the innermost reality of God's triune self, which is not a struggle between light and darkness, but a harmony of love. Darkness is no rival to the love which in Lordly freedom simply gives creation permission to be.

The Manner of Love's Coming

How shall God re-gather his wayward creation to himself? When God comes in the flesh of Jesus, we see him unashamedly eat with 'publicans and sinners' and in amazing grace forgive his enemies 'for they know not what they do' (Luke 23.34). In Jesus, the Creator redeems the promise of his unequivocal 'yes' to creation and becomes one with us, even to the point of wearing our sinful flesh. Yet God says 'no' to something. Even as God said an uncompromising 'no' to human pride in the garden of Eden, on the cross God speaks a terrible 'no' to evil's arrogance and threat that seeks to exploit and devour creation. The sacrifice of Jesus radically binds together God's utter opposition to sin with covenant tenderness toward sinners. Jesus unites in himself mercy to sinners and the final 'no' to evil in all of its guises, both blatant and hidden.

This unity is our clue to God's engagement with evil in our lives and the manner of how we are to co-labour with him in the kingdom of love; where these two things, 'no' to sin and 'yes' to the sinner, are separated, agape is absent. When I am righteously indignant at the sins of my neighbour but not compassionate, I am far from the light of agape.

> He who says he is in the light and hates his brother is still in the darkness. Whoever loves his brother lives in the light, and there is nothing in him to make him stumble. But whoever hates his brother is in the darkness and walks around in the darkness; he does not know where he is going, because the darkness has blinded him. (1 John 2.9–11).

Children of the light are not assigned the task of grumbling about the world, nor condemning it when we see its virulent vestiges in the church. Our business is to witness and celebrate the fact that the light of God shines on the world, not to destroy, but to heal.

The Warning

Let us not imagine that agape is complacent or tolerant of sin. Love's promise contains an implicit warning, namely, that 'justice shall roll down like waters and righteousness like an ever-rolling stream' (Amos 5.24), sweeping away all that aligns itself with what is false and twisted. 'The Lord is not slow about his promise as some count slowness, but is forbearing toward you, not wishing that any should perish, but that all should reach repentance' (2 Pet. 3.9). Sin is dangerous. It will devour us. It is no kindness to any sinner to be nonchalant about evil attitudes, deeds, or institutional structures. Neither pride nor promiscuity are safe and healthy alternative life-styles. The doctor who tells us not to worry about our pack-a-day habit or the dentist who does not explain to us about plaque, is neither kind nor constructive. They are not our friends; they are deceitful and negligent. A Christian who convinces himself that it is legitimate to hate one's neighbour who is ethnically and religiously different, or that sleeping with partners other than the one he is married to can be a liberation, or who increases his income on the backs of others who are made redundant or driven into poverty, is in the darkness still. Certainly the politician who appeals to our fears and greeds to rouse our patriotism is not helping us love our country.

The Intervention

Once sinners have shared his table, Pharisees have been rebuked and the feet of the disciples have been washed, how shall holy love conclusively pierce our darkness so as to heal and not obliterate? One word describes how agape unites at once this unconditional rejection of sin and the unconditional forgiveness of sinners: atonement. It is the word the publican uses in contrast to the Pharisee when he cries out to God in Jesus's parable (Luke 18.13). The root meaning is found in the Old Testament word *kippur*, the word for the covering on the mercy seat in the ark of the covenant, where the priest sprinkles blood from the innocent sacrificial lamb. In this dramatic ritual, God's holy light and our dark stain of sin touch. The blood sprinkled on the mercy seat, the kippur, at once faces with stark seriousness the darkness of evil and the healing presence of God's righteous and holy light. Only the blood of the lamb in contact with the mercy seat enables the kippur, the atonement, to occur. The huge difference in the New Testament is that Jesus Christ is not a dumb animal sacrificed in a ritual drama. If that is all Jesus is, then atonement would only be about me and my status before God. Jesus would be of no value to me apart from his use as a scapegoat. But this is not agape. Agape is not an instrument for me to use, but the coming of God himself between our evil and his holy light within our own flesh, Jesus Christ.

Atonement means God does not keep a safe, unaffected distance from evil. He touches the leprous wound, feels the sick psyche within his own person, heals us by the incarnate intimacy of he who knew no sin becoming sin for us (2 Cor. 5.21). My experience of saving love is not a status, reward, or possession but the personal communion of agape–Jesus Christ–with my sinful soul. In giving himself to us as God's lamb, Jesus is the lion of Judah whose sacrifice enacts God's unconditional love in its defining moment.

The One True Sacrifice

When a gift is given, there is usually an implicit claim in every gift. I think to myself, 'He owes me one'. I expect to receive something later, and often this results. Should I receive no reciprocation, I am disappointed. Upon further reflection I realize there is a selfish claim bound up with my gift. Only when I acknowledge this and consciously give up any claim to receive a reward in return, do I approach the realm of sacrifice. If I know and admit that I am giving myself, forgoing myself, and do not want to be repaid for it, then I have sacrificed my claim for compensation and hence a part of myself. When I fail to give up my claim for payment, my 'sacrifice' feels unsatisfactory, unrewarding.

It is upon this unacknowledged longing for recognition and compensation that our attempts at sacrificial love flounder and make the result of our 'love' unfulfilling. We wanted to give unconditionally. We thought we were, naively. But should we fail to receive the approbation we anticipated, our unresolved mental suffering forces the unwelcome discovery of how great a claim we had attached to our gift. Worse yet, we have a habit of projecting our meagre manner of giving into our theology and imagine that God gives like we do. But the Bible reveals the story of the one true sacrifice. God gave himself, on our behalf, in our place, to suffer and bear within himself the wages of sin, thus forgiving us sinners. Knowing full well we would be free to refuse the gift, denigrate it, reject it or misunderstand it, nevertheless the sacrifice is made. The gift is freely given.

And that is why God's sacrifice has its unique power to move and transform us: it is not dependent on our rewarding it with the appropriate gratitude. Jesus gives a true sacrifice, freely out of the fullness of perfect love. He is at peace in his sacrifice, not anxious whether it will be reciprocated, not worried whether preachers will call enough attention to it, or hammer it home with sufficient earnestness. He does not give in order to impress, but only to share his home in love with others, freely welcoming us to return in repentance and faith. Remember: the power of a gift's impact is directly proportional to the extent it does not assume a good return on its investment but is a free sacrifice. I grant something of myself to you for your good alone, because that in itself is reward enough. Had this not been enough, had there been an inner disposition in God that demands the gift should require a certain recognition, the result would be divine depression and unresolved suffering whenever the gift given is not properly appreciated. But the sacrifice of God arises out of the fullness of the Father and the Son, not out of a hidden need to be recognized. This is the climactic event of grace which I can only adore. The secret of praise is that we know it is not strictly necessary. God does not require it. And for that very reason, it is all the sweeter to give and for God to receive. No need for praise interferes with his pleasure in receiving.

Our faith does not win us the pardon. The pardon is the power in his sacrifice. Our repentance and faith are the response to a gift we could never earn. Here is the one sacrifice without a mixture, without a trace of bargain in it. Here is the one true and perfect sacrifice that you and I are never capable of making. That is why my trust is not in some alloy of my faith and God's sacrifice welded together. My repentance and faith look away from themselves to his sacrifice. And the more deeply I respond to the gift, and enjoy the freedom of his creativity and love, the more freely I am able to give in like manner, not as a clever investment, but in simple freedom. The Bible witnesses that here is God's way of eradicating evil while healing sinners.

Now there begins in us a lifetime of experiencing a confrontation in our lives between God's atoning mercy to us, sinners, and his holy light of love. Much to our initial, and perpetual, discomfort, our darkness is exposed. Our wishful thinking that our evil is not too serious is confronted by Jesus's total sacrifice on the cross. Because it faces our darkness, agape yields a far more comprehensive abolition of evil than a mental exercise of avoiding negative thoughts by our 'power of positive thinking'. Excuses, rationalizations, and the aggressive ignorance of our darkness are all exposed. But Jesus is our kippur, in whom a love relationship with the Father through the Spirit enters our darkness to rescue the sinner from his sin. The Spirit calls us into that agape that both exposes and judges our sins, transforming us by and through Jesus our atonement.

The Yes within the No

Agape recovers the pearl concealed in its shell of darkness, brings it to the surface, and allows the light to shine until it reflects God's glory. Consider how this differs from the Buddhist attitude toward the darkness of the world, especially if we associate darkness with strong negative emotions such as anger, fear, lust, or greed. Realizing with great clarity how profoundly damaging and destructive our passions can become, Buddhism says we purge the darkness by eradicating the passion, as we come to the insight that all earthly passions are illusory. In contrast, Jesus does not deny the reality of the darkness, but with all the tragic implications, he encounters the darkness in order to untwist and restore our passions to their true purposes. It is a matter not of unplugging our passion, but of rewiring it.

Because anger at sin is part of God's love for sinners, God's 'no' to our evil is part of his 'yes' to creation. In other words, love without judgement is idle talk. Yet grounded in God's steadfast love, this judgement is not neutral or sinister. In Dostoyevsky's *Crime and Punishment*, it is because Sonja loves Raskolnikov that she says no to his murdering of the old lady and her daughter, despite his plans to use the money to marry Sonja and develop his talents. By contrast, the police (justice without mercy) want Raskolnikov to confess also, so they can be satisfied with solving another crime and punishing the guilty. Raskolnikov is unmoved and cynical about such justice. He knows the jails are full of poor criminals while the wealthy purchase the justice necessary to minimize their damages. He is a master of alibis. Sonja's 'no' is love's rejection of all that defiles the good creation. Sonja's 'no' touches Raskolnikov to the quick because she surrounds her 'no' by the quiet covenant to bear with him the cross of travelling to Siberia and to wait for him there until he has served his entire sentence. Only this, not the merciless justice of the police, moves Raskolnikov to fall on his knees in the town square in confession.

The Ambiguity of Darkness

In our fear and anxiety to resist evil, we fail to see that the darkness that the light illumines is a compound substance and not simply demonic. That is why our resistance often becomes counter-productive. Evil weaves together our wounds and our wickedness, our honest needs and our dishonest greeds. It includes undeveloped parts of us, things ignored, things humiliated, things devalued. This explains our difficulty in rooting evil out. It is a convoluted mixture of rejection and revenge, anger and hate, victim and victimizer, which becomes the shadowy breeding ground where deeper shades of darkness are woven. In the dark, separated from holy love, this mixture becomes a phantom empire of egotism and error. When only the candle of my egotism interprets and directs my passions, the combustion of hurt plus anger plus egotism erupts into deeds of cumulative cruelty.

When the light of the gospel exposes this guilty darkness, the pain of this exposure can be startling. Yet the refiner's fire of agape heals as it burns, consuming and melting distorted personality arrangements which, untutored by holy love, have been formed down in the darkness. In *The Great Divorce*, the ghost with a lizard of lust on his shoulder hates and is ashamed of his disgusting companion. Yet he is so lonely and afraid to be without it, that for the angel to kill it seems inseparable from killing himself. Granting the angel permission to perform this spiritual surgery is the most painful and courageous act of his life. More than matching the pain of its departure is the joy at the lizard's transformation into a noble horse. 'But it was killed first.'[3]

Without Hate or Fear

To be redeemed, darkness must be pitied. No one has expressed this better than J. R. R. Tolkien as he describes how the hobbit, Frodo, mercifully spares the wretched, treacherous Gollum's life. In a way utterly unanticipated, his act of pity enables the ring of evil power to be destroyed. The swords and armour of the great kingdoms warring on the battlefield are as nothing compared with the silent struggle of Frodo and Sam, shadowed by Gollum, venturing in the darkness along Mount Doom. Had Frodo acted out of his fear or hate, he would never have received Gollum's paradoxical help in his own anguished moment of failure and weakness.

Evil intimidates us by flaunting its power. And Christians can be too impressed by evil's publicity campaign and tell exorcist 'ghost stories' to their children in order to frighten them into commitment, or at least better behaviour. But when evil inflates its prowess, it creates the conditions for its own fall. Love calls its bluff and dares to believe that justice mingled with mercy and grace is stronger. Somewhere Ignatius says, 'If you feel the presence of the demonic and you approach it faithfully and aggressively, it shrinks. If you run from it, it becomes a ferocious lion that pursues you.' Tolkien writes to his son during wartime: 'All we do know, and that to a large extent by direct experience, is that evil labours with vast power and perpetual success–in vain; preparing always only the soil for unexpected good to sprout in. So it is in general, and so it is in our own lives. . . .'[4] As we grow in confidence that even 'the wrath of men shall praise him' (Ps. 76.10), that God's sovereign love is able to use even the greatest evil to work out his purposes, our anxiety about evil's power lessens, and our temptation to ape its strategies, diminishes.

Unexpected Weapons

God's methods in Christ do not change when evil confronts Christians today. Evil is not destroyed by light-sabre-wielding angels. The temptation to overwhelm and dominate through power is what Jesus refused. Let us arrange a moratorium on violent metaphors to describe the victory of the gospel over evil. Their inspiration comes more from Stephen King or 'Rambo' than the light which shines from Calvary. Because our humanity is so entwined by evil, God's fallen creation is not a monochrome sulphureous black target for divine missiles and tanks. Our dreams and hopes are caged within our hatreds and fears. Around this complex prison evil tries to weave a spider's web of seamless darkness. But we must not fall prey to this demonic ruse by imagining the darkness as simply all black. This blinds us from glimpsing that what is caught in the web is precious and has been imprisoned. When we adopt a scorched earth policy of search and destroy, when we label our enemies as evil, our own evil has seduced the children of light to act with the panic of the bludgeon. In contrast, the *shalom* of God uses the Great Physician's scalpel of mercy and judgement in atonement, thus disentangling us from evil's web. I am not suggesting there is not an irreducibly demonic element, but the *blitzkrieg* approach smashes the hidden pearl. It energizes the latent self-righteousness within us to strike out at a target which will require no further repentance on our part, no further confrontation with our own darkness.

In the darkness of Good Friday, the lethal combination of proud ignorance, hatred, and fear apparently extinguishes the light of God. Not destroyed, but only hidden, the light descends into the heart of darkness in order to bring deliverance to the spirits in prison (1 Pet. 3.19). No laser beams of power. No horsemen of Mohammad with swords drawn to massacre the enemy as they ride to claim Mecca. This king rides to face his enemies on a donkey with children strewing his way with palm branches, shouting praises. He marches as to war, armed only with a sword inverted to make a cross.

Unavoidably, the transformation of fear and hate to pity and forgiveness has personal coefficients. Years later, after preaching throughout Europe and America on forgiveness, Corrie Ten Boom must face that very prison guard who inflicted great cruelty on her and her sister. That parent, husband, friend or sister who betrayed you waits beside you, and inside you, to receive your pardon. For love to be formed within our inner structures of personality, a crucifixion of pride and the desire to punish must be undergone. But for the joy that love anticipates, we endure the cross.

Resist Not Evil?

How did Jesus know when to tell Peter 'Get behind me, Satan', or when to turn over the money-changer's tables, yet before Pilate to be as dumb as a lamb at the slaughter, and later to allow his enemies to get so close, he permits the lash, the mockery, and the crucifixion? 'But I say to you, Do not resist one who is evil. But if any one strikes you on the right cheek, turn to him the other also . . .' (Matt. 5.39). Let us assume that Jesus is not advocating that we make the police redundant so bullies can roam the streets exploiting victims. If we do not protect children against teachers like Wackford Squeers we are cowards and enablers of abuse, recipients of the woe that Jesus speaks to those who allow little ones to be tempted to sin (Matt. 18.6). The gift of forgiveness does not cancel out the reality that evil deeds have consequences. The person corrupted by his lies cannot be healed inside by our forgiveness unless he faces his radical need of mercy implicit in the pardon of grace. As with St Paul, the measure of our healing and participation in the forgiveness given will be our hunger to put right and to make reparation where yet possible.

Let us state this in a social context. The need for prison

reform along Christian principles is urgent. There is no denying there are criminals who must be separated from the public for the sake of everyone's safety. Jesus's words 'resist not evil' haunt us when we fence evil-doers in with bricks and mortar and leave them to sit and rot. What does this strategy accomplish? Britain keeps a greater percentage of its population in jail than any other nation in Europe. The United States, which has the highest percentage of its population in the world behind bars, spends over $35,000 per year per prisoner, more than it costs to send a young person to an excellent university. Yet in spite of huge investments in punishment, our crime rates increase and our prison populations grow at record rates. It seems the more we hate and fear evil, the more we punish it, the more evil thrives on our hatred and fear. The very place where evil is supposedly walled in and controlled becomes a graduate school for repeat offenders.

Then there is the 'peace-keeping' strategy of retaliation. This theory argues that we overcome the evil out there by stockpiling, and strategically using, weapons to intimidate, threaten and if need be, annihilate our adversary. This philosophy has granted immense influence to the weapons' merchants around the globe, so much so that many nations, including Britain and America, spend half of their yearly budgets just on defence: weapons, research, personnel. Far more than half of all university-trained scientists, our brightest and best, are employed in defence-related industry. In the 1980s America's appetite for defence went on such a binge that it tripled its budget deficit, creating an immense structural barrier to the healthy growth of the economy. Some third world nations have bankrupted their countries buying arms from Western nations eager to export. In recent UN military actions in the Gulf and Somalia, we witnessed the bizarre spectacle of UN troops being attacked by weapons which had been sold by these same UN nations. In Somalia, though food was scarce, weapons from Western exporters were in such abundance they, ironically, posed the major threat to food distribution. I am not suggesting that we can or should simply shut down the military and defence departments. Obviously improved regulation in the sale and distribution of weapons is long overdue. But even more urgently, the energy we now expend to retaliate and build defences against aggression cries out to be baptized into a new approach to our adversary. Jesus unveils a very different strategy for his disciples in the unique warfare whereby soldiers of the cross internalize the way of the cross to redeem evil. Jesus invites us on a narrow path between the revenge spiral and acquiescence.

Today at home and at work we shall receive another's aggression in words or in deeds. What shall we do? Curl up in a ball, and do nothing but inwardly boil? Storm out of the room and slam the door? Hit back, reasoning that the best defence is a good offence? The logic of retaliation opens the door to the nightmares of the Lebanons, the Northern Irelands, the Croat-Serbian spirals of revenge. Walking away until our pre-conditions are agreed to leads to divorce and abandonment. Our absolute pre-conditions are countered by our adversary's own. Everyone dreads the thought of being dominated by the other. These seem to be our choices–all bad.

Let us recall that the darkness of sin is not unambiguous. Human evil results from hungers and thirsts that have not been and are not being met. Out of this mixture of hurt, loneliness, rage, and fear arises evil. It multiplies as we grasp after and stuff down false nutrients. The question is: do we wish to destroy our enemy or see him healed? Destroying is easy. Call down the legions of angels. Imagine them with their light-sabres piercing the darkness. This is the overly pious letting off a bit of spiritual steam. When it is the military with loaded ammunition, not the angels, the piety is more blatantly bogus. Peter was told to put up his sword if he was to be a healer, not an enforcer.

The problem is that when evil attacks, it activates our own evil, our own mix of indignation and fear. 'How dare they? Don't they know, or care, who I am?' Pride and fear pump fire in our veins. If we swallow this fire, we repress and simmer in silence or simply avoid by flight. We hate ourselves for being cowardly. We plan to punish by separation. If we resist and belch out our fire, we hope to destroy our adversary, or at least to give a bit better than we get. But the sum total of evil only increases. Welcome to a little piece of Lebanon, Bosnia, Belfast, or whatever you care to name it, right here in your personal neighbourhood.

There is another way. Evil attacks, usually unexpectedly, with a mocking word, a cruel blow. As the panic of our flight or fight reactions starts to kick in, what if, instead of defending or attacking, which ignite the flames, we relax, and allow the action to sweep through our mind and our body? What if we swallow the experience, drink it down, and not refuse the bitter cup?

What if we abide with someone, without rejecting them, despite their attack? What if their aggression is not resisted and defended against, what then? What if we can stay undefended, unattacking, for a moment longer, and lean into the pain, descending further, past the anger, past the critical spirit, the harshness? We emerge into a new dimension of life. We are travelling, quite unexpectedly, along a bridge into our enemy's inner soul of hurt, anger and deprivation. We are journeying through the barriers of protection and protest into something deeper, something hidden and hurting. If we venture a bit further, we enter virgin territory of pain and inflammation. We shall be near something raw, untended, and infected. It is but a glimpse of the abuse, the hurt my adversary lives within and suffers moment by moment. If we can manage to stay here long enough to know something of their inner life, and not reject or fight, we have the great joy and honour of planting the smallest flag of love there in that deserted and abscessed place.

As with each encounter with evil, there is mystery here. We cannot imagine taking this narrow path between punishment and rejection unless someone has first so loved us. Even then we cannot stay for very long. We must come out for fresh air, so toxic is the atmosphere. To enter there is no soft alternative to revenge or rejection. It is a crucifying experience to descend to this place. Some part of our own character and our own woundedness must merge into the baptism of Christ on the cross to come this far and not to reject or seek revenge. With whatever degree of maturity and intimacy, with a solemn covenant to do no harm, to take no advantage, we offer love unexpectedly, penetrating where aggression or fear usually protects against any such vulnerability. When this happens, in some small way we have journeyed with someone into the infected epicentre of their injury. We cannot stay for long both for our own sake, but also because we might be falsely gripped with grandiose presumptions of our permanence and our love could degenerate into dominance over a broken brother or sister. We cannot stay for long because it would violate the other rule of combat for soldiers of the cross, that each of us must also bear our own cross and this too is vital to redemption. I can only bear it with you for a moment, though perhaps with the support of and accountability to a community, I can return again as a soul friend.

Only Jesus goes all the way down with us, descending past the rage, the humiliation, the terrifying loneliness, descending into

the ultimate fear, the hell of abandonment itself. He comes there
not to reject nor to destroy. He embraces the ashamed, frightened, and furious soul and comes with the triumphant battle cry,
'Father, it is finished!' He sets the captives free.

When you and I are soldiers of the cross, his battle becomes
our blueprint: not to curse sinners but to bless them. It is the
front-line work of reconciliation. But as we do this basic work of
taking up our little cross and following, we discover more about
ourselves than we wanted to know, more about our own angers,
hungers, fears and hurts. Why? Because these become constel-
lated, no longer quietly dormant, but reactivated and inflamed
when we enter the battle of 'Thy kingdom come'. Much to our
humiliation, with no respect for our visions of spiritual grandeur,
our adversaries expose the cavernous dimensions of our own
wounds. They disclose how our weakness has hidden itself behind
a strength. More than ever intended, we become acquainted
with our own need to be embraced and strengthened by Christ's
descending, shame-scattering love. Yet a new song of praise arises
also, for in these experiences we feel a new part of ourselves
alive again which we had thought dead. Our own hope, faith,
and love increase as we no longer defend, pretend, and posture
lest that self is exposed and rejected: 'And with his stripes we are
healed.' As more of us have these inner experiences, we will have
increasing confidence to extend a new kind of passion, let us call
it compassion, outward to our neighbours and adversaries.

Meanwhile we pray for discernment when to do the prelimi-
nary work of overthrowing evil tables, rebuking the Peters, and
when the time is right to toil in the serious yet simple work of
sacrificial love. As we pray for such wisdom, we ask God to cleanse
our own hearts that we might use sacrifice only for love's sake to
set other people free to be His children, not for us to have power
over others or create clones. And we must not forget that when
we engage in heaven's warfare against evil, He is our rock, our
high tower, our hiding place in the most awkward and hopeless
situations. Especially in those places.

The Outer Enemy

But I say to you, Love your enemies and pray for those who
persecute you, so that you may be sons of your Father who
is in heaven . . . For if you love those who love you, what
reward have you? Do not even the tax collectors do the same?

(Mt. 5.44, 46). Bless those who persecute you; bless and do not curse them . . . Repay no one evil for evil . . . if your enemy is hungry, feed him; if he is thirsty give him drink . . . Do not be overcome by evil, but overcome evil with good. (Rom. 12.14, 17, 20, 21)

If we take these words as orders for our emotions, they become entangled in the same road-blocks as other orders to our feelings such as 'Be thankful!', 'Be happy!', 'Love your enemies!' But Jesus is not giving us mood commands, he is showing us the way in which reconciliation is possible in the real world. He forthrightly acknowledges the true situation, that they are not friends, but enemies. Of course when we are seething with anger, to put these words into practice is the greatest challenge of living the way of love. But let us realize that when attacked by an enemy, the anger we feel racing inside us is of a piece with the rage which led the evil act of cruelty or terrorism to be first performed. Those who planned and planted the bomb on the Pan Am flight over Lockerbie were first outraged at the mistaken downing of the civilian Iranian passenger jet. The agent of evil in attacking us, infects us with his own callousness or fury. That is why the victim so easily slides into the role of victimizer.

The Enemy Within

One of the baffling things about loving our enemies is discovering who in fact is our enemy. We confuse ourselves by our unconscious preference to project the inner atmosphere of our internalized domestic conflict management style, accumulated from our previous years, into our present conflicts. As we have seen, there is an inner amplification system we bring along from childhood. A small mother may have kept order at home among four bruising lads by the tone of her voice, the click of her tongue, and the shaking of her head. No need to shout or use force. By the time we are adults we may have an amplifying system that spots our faults and errors so sensitively that if our woofers and tweeters could be adjusted for music, they could use our system at a Wembley rock-concert. Suppose the boss, or a colleague, or our partner comments on something we have left undone or on some positive sin of commission. Suppose they thought they mentioned it rather casually or as a matter of fact, but we feel stung to the quick. If our critic is our wife, we may begin feeling toward her the way we felt toward our mother when she scolded us and told us we were naughty. We begin to turn her into a mother we must pacify or alternatively, whinge at, not as an equal with whom we can converse, share our life, and explore mutual adaptations. We see her as a threat, as our enemy. But who is the real enemy? Is it the wife or the inner amplifier wherein our mother's or father's worst attribute– harshness, shaming–is a permanent part of our reception system?

My outer enemy may be my room-mate, my political opponent, or the elders of my church. But what if my rage or my emotional divorce is misguided? Then Jesus gives us the very practical advice to love and pray for that one with whom we are in conflict. In prayer I bring my rage or desire for revenge into the Father's presence: 'Why did that comment about my work hurt so and make me panic inside? Why did his silence frighten me? What wound or hurt is this touching? Why should my boss's threat make me feel paralysed and helpless? Was it a genuine threat or is my old inner stereo-system too finely tuned once more?'

Praying in this exploratory way before the Father, turns my adversary or persecutor into an undercover agent who leads me to the place where my inner sound-system is either flat or sharp. There in prayer, I do not run away or attack. I bring the conflict into the Father's presence and explore where the true tension lies, hidden but inflamed once again and crippling my relationships in the present. By the end of the prayer session, I may be praying for a different enemy.

> Charles had spent his childhood with a parent whose own tragic story had left her constantly needing attention, anticipating crises, and demanding help. With the absence of father, the role fell to Charles to play 'Jim'll fix it'. He spent his childhood pleasing or trying to please mother. It got so he was attuned to anticipate problems and solve them almost before she noted them herself. Upon marrying, this lifelong pattern began to re-emerge. Whenever his wife had a problem with the cooker, with the garden, with her boss, with her family, and so on, instantly he was out with the tool-kit repairing, down to the DIY shop getting a replacement, giving a pep talk on what to tell the boss or her parents. Still tuned into the old sound-system, he was interpreting his present life through the sounds of the past. At first it was natural enough for his wife to play along. But he was growing weary. Underneath was

the anger of resenting having to always be 'Jim'll fix it'. He was angry too because according to the unwritten rules of this game, there was never anyone to fix it for him. It is not always fun being married to 'Jim'll fix it' either. Some things cannot be 'fixed'. Sometimes you may forget to be grateful for all the effort at fixing. This arouses the fixer's wrath.

Who was the enemy? His wife or the inner sound-system through which he *heard* his wife's concerns, his employer's requests and his children's complaints? As we pray for our beloved enemy, we learn to separate out and pray for the dominant parent-image (a negative idealization albeit based on reality) that we brought with us into the present relationship. We learn to ask who was there to help us in our hours of need and why did we become so adept at helping others and not attending to our own goals and longings. We take time to grieve the absence of care when we were so busy caring for others. We learn not to curse our enemies, gradually, over time. We learn to do this in prayer and sharing with a spiritually mature friend, pastor, or therapist who does not panic at our emotions. And we find that our outer enemy has led us to discover with clarity the interior wounds we have repressed and 'forgotten'. Praying for our outer enemy leads us to face our inner enemy: 'God, part of me is hounded by an over-controlling, nagging voice. This voice is making it impossible for me to be close to others. This voice is an inner part of me! How do I love and forgive this inner part of me that always finds fault, always is dissatisfied?' The Gospel tells us to bring this hurt and anger out of the darkness into the light. Having let the light of grace shine upon this old enemy, we can ask for eyes of forgiveness. Then we walk back to our outer enemy, the one who turned on the alarm activating the old system, in a new way.

Rarely is the decisive encounter with our enemy exclusively internal or external. As we bring our outer enemies before the Lord in prayer, we discover our anger or fear was once love and respect that became hurt, was left unprotected and brutalized. As I pray for my enemy, I actually inquire with God into two areas: I ask for the eyes of forgiveness to see the fearful or anxious person within the person who persecutes me; then I pray for the wisdom to trace within my own soul the sound-system that has amplified to the point of anguish the deeds and words of my outer enemy. In this process of prayer, I learn how neither to attack nor to run away, but to stay alongside. I learn not to take my outer enemy's blame or anger at face value, knowing it too has a prior history.

As we open ourselves to the gospel possibility of loving our enemies and praying for them, it will change the way we listen to our politicians. Instead of nodding our heads in agreement when, for example, the former Soviet Union is called 'the evil empire' we shall notice how the Soviet quest for power and influence has struck a huge amplifying note in our own heart. And the reason we hear it so loudly and react so strongly and drive our military spending up so dramatically when we see it out there is because the urge for power and dominance, and the anxious fear of conquest, is the unacknowledged cancer shadowing our own agenda. And our indignation and impatience at the little dictators may not be as noble as we once thought. Expanding the habit of prayer for our enemies to international relations, opens new possibilities that negotiations based on mercy and justice may increasingly replace our reptilian preference for military solutions.

Meanwhile, in our little corner of the universe we begin to feel the pride-scattering power of love course through our lives as we stand alongside our beloved enemies. And no one is a lost cause because God has loved his enemies in Jesus Christ:

> And when he had taken the scroll, the four living creatures and the twenty-four elders fell down before the Lamb, each holding a harp, and with golden bowls full of incense, which are the prayers of the saints; and they sang a new song, saying, 'Worthy art thou to take the scroll and to open its seals, for thou wast slain and by thy blood didst ransom men for God from every tribe and tongue and people and nation, and hast made them a kingdom and priests to our God, and they shall reign on earth'. (Rev. 5.8–10).

Notes

1 Quoted in Malcolm Muggeridge, *Christ and the Media*, (Grand Rapids: Eerdmans, 1977), p. 46.

2 Hannah Arendt, *Eichmann in Jerusalem*, (New York: Penguin, [1963], 1977), p. 26.

3 C. S. Lewis, *The Great Divorce*, (New York: Macmillan, [1946], 1973), p. 99.

4 J. R. R. Tolkien, *Letters*, (London: Allen and Unwin, 1981), p. 46.

Index of Subjects and Names

Index of Biblical References